The Singer's Companion

The Singer's Companion

A Guide to Improving Your Voice and Performance

By Brent Jeffrey Monahan

Published in 2006 by Limelight Editions
512 Newark Pompton Turnpike
Pompton Plains, New Jersey 07444

Printed in the United States of America

Book design by Kristina Rolander
Illustrations by Cliff Mott
Music typesetting by Staccato Media Group Inc.

Library of Congress Cataloging-in-Publication Data is available upon request.

ISBN 1-57467-150-2

Grateful acknowledgment is made to the following:

Carl Fischer, LLC, which on behalf of Oliver Ditson Company (Theodore Presser Company) granted permission for the use of previously published material: Excerpt from *Fundamentals of Voice Training* by D. A. Clippinger, copyright, MCMXXIX, by Oliver Ditson Company. International Copyright Secured. Excerpts from *The Clippinger Class-Method of Voice Culture* by D. A. Clippinger, copyright, MCMXXXII, by Oliver Ditson Company. Reprinted with permission.

Indiana University Press, which granted permission to reproduce Figure 14 from *The Science of Vocal Pedagogy* by D. Ralph Appelman.

www.limelighteditions.com

Contents

Introduction

WHY USE THIS BOOK?

The Singer's Companion is designed for the singing teacher and for any student serious about improving both vocal quality and performance. This is not a scientific textbook that focuses on singing physiology and acoustics or theories of phonation but rather a highly practical set of tools that offer only what may help the performer sing better. A treasure trove of wisdom is packed into this volume. Although my name alone is on the cover, this book results from the combined insights of hundreds of history's best singers and singing teachers.

In Western civilization, the first manuscripts discussing singing date from about 1200 AD. Since then, in Europe and North America, thousands of singing books have been published. Scarecrow Press published John Carroll Burgin's *Teaching Singing,* which analyzed the published thoughts on singing from just 1943 to 1973. Burgin lists and draws quotations from 141 books (including reprints of previous editions) and more than a thousand magazine and journal articles. All of these barely touch on information published in languages other than English during that period. This book and books by Phillip Duey (*Bel Canto in Its Golden Age* [New York: King's Crown Press, 1951]), Victor Alexander Fields (*Training the Singing Voice* [New York: King's Crown Press, 1947]), and me (*The Art of Singing: A Compendium of Thoughts on Singing Published Between 1777 and 1927* [Metuchen, NJ: Scarecrow Press, 1978]) have sought to analyze and codify the thoughts of thousands of professionals on singing. They contain wonderful extracts, but they are reference books. None is a practical singing companion. Certainly, the sources they quote are almost all out of print and so widely disbursed that it is too much trouble for the average singer to hunt for them. I first collected the material of this book for my students. It proved so productive that I felt it should be offered to a broader audience.

I am not interested in making you read any more than you need to for the sake of padding. This book is, therefore, as condensed as I can make it without omitting essential information. It is as packed with benefit as a bottle of vitamin pills. It is truly intended to be a resource companion or vademecum.

The objective of this book is not to make you sing freely but to let you sing freely, in complete mastery of your vocal mechanism and your artistic goals. It is not intended to complicate but rather to simplify, not to clutter up but to clear away. Be assured that singing, properly mastered, is not a difficult physical act. It is wholly natural. I should also emphasize that this book is meant not only for the classical but also for the musical theater, pop, and everyday singer.

In a way, this book is a primer on self-organization. You already have every bit of equipment you need to sing well. However, if you are like I was as a student, you are like a room filled with items important to life but in such a jumble that you can't get at them.

WHY RELY ON ME TO CHOOSE THE INFORMATION IN THIS BOOK?

Too many singing books I have read fail to list the writer's qualifications, but I believe these are helpful, if only to make the reader feel his or her money, time, and confidence will not be misspent. Here are mine:

I studied singing formally for twenty years. My first teacher, Harry Roger Naylor of Trenton, New Jersey, was an original Edison recording artist and a coach of one American tour of the D'Oyly Carte Company (of Gilbert and Sullivan operetta fame). Also, to quote a pamphlet on him, he was "a Teacher to a Conductor of the Berlin Opera" and a professional concert singer who credited living to the age of ninety-eight partially to being a professional breather.

I have decades of experience singing professionally, from opera to cabaret. This experience dates back to age eleven, when I was a boy soprano.

I have formally worked with or observed at work more than a dozen vocal coaches, including Walter Cassel, Eileen Farrell, and Margaret Harshaw, all of Metropolitan Opera fame. Harshaw's coaching placed pupils in the finals of Metropolitan Opera auditions almost every year she taught. I have observed excellent, fair, and poor teachers and have witnessed the various results of their methods.

My doctoral dissertation, *The Art of Singing*, was in print for many years. It serves as the 1777–1927 component of several standard reference compendiums already listed concerning knowledge on legitimate singing. Creating this volume required me to analyze more than 160 widely used books on improving the singing voice.

I hold a doctor of musical arts degree "with high distinction" from Indiana University, Bloomington, in vocal pedagogy—that is, teaching the singing voice. The School of Music in the period before and after my attendance was internationally regarded as the top vocal school in the world.

I have personally employed the wisdom in this book, teaching scores of students over a thirty-year period and helping them solve many vocal problems. Moreover, many students possessed nearly identical weaknesses and bad habits. The list of vocal concerns is not limitless. For this reason, your difficulties will probably be touched on here.

My students have gone on to take leading roles and soloist parts in many semiprofessional and professional productions. Several have won substantial scholarships to colleges, and a few have earned places in national programs that admit extremely few students.

How to Use This Book

First, read it front to back. After that, consult it selectively. It is organized by topic, and the most important information is offered in **boldface**. Don't skip much, because I have cut out most of the fat already. I have omitted a great deal of the science and mechanics of singing required for a university singing degree because most people merely want to sing well and are not interested in all the science and minutiae. Airline pilots do not need to know every aspect of the physics and engineering of an airplane to fly one well. I sympathize with a pragmatic attitude in this busy world, especially if you intend singing only as an avocation.

About the Teaching of Singing

In Western civilization, there exist records of so-called experts teaching others to sing for at least 400 years. This teaching, therefore, began long before the era of scientific investigation. Hundreds of years ago, just as today, a rare number of people existed who naturally sang beautifully, powerfully, freely, and with no signs of tiring or harming their vocal apparatus. This is a gift of nature or the Creator, if they can be separated. Wishing to obtain the same gifts by study and practice, others questioned and carefully observed these singers. This observation-based approach has come to be known as the *empirical method,* as opposed to the later-emerging *scientific method.* The observers found certain practices to be common among good singers and, in time, their findings began to be collected into books and pamphlets or passed on verbally by instruction from generation to generation. My first teacher, for example, was born in 1872 (I was his last pupil). He learned from people performing during the end of the bel canto period (in Italian, *bel canto* means "beautiful singing"). This often-used term curiously was not popular during its supposed period, which is around 1750–1850 and may stretch back further, depending on who is consulted. Much of what these empirical pupils learned had been collected as aphorisms of the "A penny saved is a penny earned" variety, and I shall pass them along to you.

Careful observation, in fact, eventually yielded all the truths necessary to develop perfect or near-perfect singers. This success can be proven by the difficulty of the vocal music written during this time. About 1860, advances in science were overlaid on this knowledge. People wondered if more truths might be learned about this somewhat mysterious art form, to distribute the gift more widely and to simplify that process. One of the greatest teachers of singing, Manuel Garcia the younger, had himself been trained and had sung professionally, and had taught by the empirical method for quite a while, before he developed the laryngoscope to observe the sound-making human mechanism directly. All that this scientific discovery accomplished was to help describe the function behind truths that he already knew.

I have read hundreds of pamphlets, books, and scholarly articles on scientific aspects of what makes for beautiful singing, and although much of their content seemed correct, they did not produce an explosion of excellent singers. To tell a soprano that the laws of physics make virtually impossible the intelligibility of certain vowels above 700 vibrations per second does not allow her to overcome the law. Rather, centuries ago, necessity resulted in singers developing *quality vowel modifications*. This was sufficient to solve the problem.

Therefore, because I ascribe to the sayings "Old ways are the best ways" and "If it ain't broke, don't fix it," I will generally offer the classical approach developed from about 1650 to 1900. This is why you will see that eighteenth- and nineteenth-century quotations dominate the book. When asked by a Roman officer if he could summarize the teachings of Judaism while standing on one leg, the great ancient scholar Hillel said, "Love God and love your neighbor; all the rest is commentary." Many books and articles written in the twentieth century are correct and useful, but from my point of view they are commentary on, expansion of, and proof of the truths earlier discovered.

PREREQUISITES

For this book to have any value to you, it makes several assumptions. The first is that you have the power of speech. Here is your first Old Italian Master aphorism (from Pacchiarotti, 1744–1821): "He who knows how to breathe and pronounce correctly knows well how to sing."

This saying makes several assumptions of its own. The major one is my second assumption: that you are not tone-deaf. In other words, if someone plays a note in your range on a piano, you are able to match it, and if two tones are played on a piano, you can correctly identify with your ears which pitch is higher.

A further assumption is that for this book to have any value for you, you cannot merely read it but must also put the concepts and exercises into practice. The mind must connect with the body and form good habits. To help you, a CD with exercises, sample songs, and common errors and their corrections is included.

You will also need to have access to a mirror, so that you can observe yourself while singing. This mirror, optimally, should be large enough and placed so that you can observe from your eyes to your belly button while looking straight forward.

Eventually, you should place your trust in a competent vocal coach. I will state reasons later in this book. The main one, objectivity, has to do with the poet Robert Burns's famous lines *"Ah wad sum power the giftee gie us / To see ourselves as ithers see us"* [Oh, what power to have the gift of being able to see ourselves as others see us]. You will not be surprised to have me advise you to present this book or some of the most important admonitions from this book to your prospective teacher and to ask for comment. If you are pleased by the teacher's responses and they seem to make sense to you (whether or not the person agrees with everything in this book), then you will want to trust yourself to his or her care, at least until you can judge if you are improving.

METHOD

In this guide, I both present what you should do and justify why you should do it. Almost nothing of what I am presenting is mine or revolutionary. I stand on the shoulders of many distinguished predecessors who have struggled toward good singing, and I quote them liberally. In some cases, I will tell you where professionals have differed in their opinions on aspects of singing, tell you which opinion I believe to be better, and let you make up your own mind. This approach will often seem to come from Monty Python's Office of Redundancy Office, because I think up my words so often with those of writers who published previously successful singing books. However, my purpose is not only to justify my points of view by appealing to outside authority, but also to use on you the tried-and-true U.S. Army training method of "Tell 'em what you're gonna tell 'em; tell 'em; then tell 'em what you just told 'em."

A second reason for redundancy is that I write this book with the subjective opinion that everything I espouse makes common sense. Nothing you read should seem illogical to you. However, in case my failure to provide fitting words is the cause of your doubt or confusion, I have also placed the observations of other teachers below my contentions so you may grasp the ideas through different descriptions.

You will also find that I have repeated some quotations in separate parts of the text. I have done this because the wisdom applies in both places, and also so that you will not have to thumb through the entire book to find a pertinent thought when you want to use it for reference.

Please be aware that many of the accomplished teachers of singing I quote were not necessarily also transparent writers. They committed errors in grammar, punctuation, and spelling that their editors overlooked, chose to ignore, or were unaware of themselves (or, in some instances, these mistakes were considered correct at the time of publication). I elected not to correct these mistakes. However, every once in a while you will see me stepping in to comment on or to try to explain or guess what the author meant. In these cases, my comments will be included in square brackets [], which indicate that I'm making a minor correction or I'm talking to you inside the quotation.

I approach good singing from a commonly used and logical, step-by-step method — that is, first stance, then breathing. This is the "You must crawl, then walk before you can run" approach. I often attempt to simplify complex ideas by using analogies that can be easily converted and pictured in the mind. I hope you agree that the more vivid an image, the more easily it is grasped and assimilated. For example, I regularly compare the singing voice to the automobile. The car has become a machine that almost every adult owns, yet it has many more implications than merely getting us and whatever else we want to transport from point A to point B. Given the choice between a rattletrap junker that barely moves and a beautifully designed luxury car with quick acceleration, deft handling, and comfort, everyone wants the latter rather than the former.

Similarly, virtually everyone can sing. This does not mean they sing well. What we want to do is tantamount to taking an everyday car and—by providing a detailed owner's manual for understanding care and use (the mental element) and retuning, repainting, and polishing it (the physical element)—gradually transforming handling and appearance. The result of this process is something that others will admire and that will give us great satisfaction, performance, and personal pleasure with maximum comfort and minimum trouble for many years.

Singing is a psychophysical art. The brain, consciously or unconsciously, instructs the body what to do to create musical sound. We all know how complex the brain is. We all also know how notoriously unreliable words are in getting knowledge into the brain, especially knowledge that must become a physical act. Therefore, I will try to offer several images for each aspect of good singing, in the hope that at least one of them may provide an improvement for you.

I begin with the mechanics of good singing and then tackle the artistic aspects. This is because, frankly, few people other than your relatives will want to listen to you, no matter how artistically you sing, if your voice is breathy, throaty, flat, or strained. Again frankly, a person who is not in command of her or his voice simply cannot perform many artistic elements, such as singing a long phrase that should not have breaths in the middle or reaching "high" notes without cracking.

Just as the instruction manual on any complex instrument or appliance contains a "What to do when this thing doesn't work" diagnostic section in the rear, I will provide this as well in early sections.

In an effort to compel the singer toward better singing tones and methods, thousands of vocal exercises and vocalises have been developed over the centuries. In searching through hundreds of books, I have observed that some common exercises are used by many wise teachers. I have borrowed and included these, along with an explanation of why they work and what they are intended to accomplish.

Finally, for the rare person who wants to explore the sources used, or for the doubting Thomas who must verify citations, I provide bibliographic information.

The Singer's Companion

PART I

The Mechanics of Singing

CHAPTER 1

$\mathcal{S}$tance

THE ELEMENTS

THE SINGER NEEDS TO HAVE AN INTEGRATED, balanced support system in place before beginning to sing. This is accomplished by the bones and muscles, directed by the brain.

The importance of this support system can be illustrated by using my favored automobile analogy, as discussed in the Introduction. There isn't any car unless it has a framework, which is called the *chassis*. The engine, transmission, tires, steering, all have to be held together so that they can perform as one. Moreover, after 100,000 miles, when bolts and welds have worked loose, the owner can definitely feel how much less comfortable the ride is, as the chassis is no longer firmly assembled.

Important Note:

Never do anything advocated in this book in a forceful, tense, or strained manner. The mark of any great performer, artistic or athletic, is that she or he makes the effort look so easy that an audience might think anyone could do it. The tightrope walker and the ballerina accomplish their acts by balance and not brute strength. It is the same with singing.

According to Edmund J. Myer in the eighth edition (so it must have resonated with many would-be singers and their teachers) of his *Position and Action in Singing:*

But few singers understand and use correct position and action in singing, and yet they are absolutely necessary to the full development and use of all the powers of the singer. Right singing means a free, flexible, elastic action of the entire body, and free, natural, automatic form and action of the mouth and throat; it means correct bodily action and position, that which is called "**The singer's position.**"

There must be elasticity of movement, expansion and firmness, the result of correct position, but never rigidity, the result of contraction. There must be bodily harmony throughout; which means coordination of the body and vocal muscles, each complementing and assisting the others through correct flexible position and action. There is a wonderful sympathy between the body and throat muscles in singing. (1911, 32)

Good singing is 90 percent mental and 10 percent physical.

Figure 1 provides a side view of the human form in its optimal stance for singing. Likewise, the following list enumerates some of the specific features of optimal stance.

FIGURE 1

The human form, seen from the side

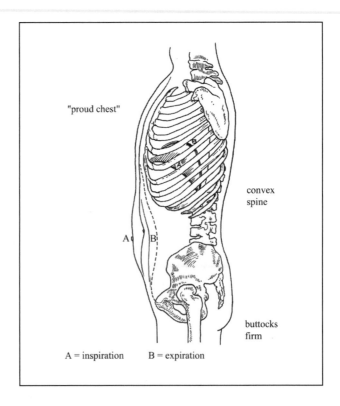

"proud chest"

convex spine

buttocks firm

A = inspiration   B = expiration

1. **Stand up straight.** Standing is the optimal position for good singing, because it is easier to breathe standing.

2. **One foot in front of the other.** Place one foot about the distance of the foot in front of the other. Leave a little space between the feet. Place about 65 percent of the weight on the leading foot. Feel the weight of the body on the toes and the ball of the front foot. The great Italian tenor Caruso said that he was sure that if he ever lost his toes he would no longer be able to sing. The celebrated coloratura soprano Joan Sutherland was noted for rising on her toes when she hit very high notes, so intent was she on a forward position.

    If you look down while in this position, you will realize that a line between the toes of the two feet forms the hypotenuse of a triangle. The triangle is a very stable geometric shape. In this case, it will prevent the kind of swaying and imbalance made famous by the Tin Woodman in the movie version of *The Wizard of Oz* when he stands on the Yellow Brick Road.

3. **If the leading foot gets tired, advance the other foot.** In performance, do this by stepping forward with the trailing foot, as this is received by the audience as wanting to be closer rather than shrinking from them.

4. **Keep the legs straight without locking them. Especially do not lock your knees.**

5. **Use the buttocks to hold yourself up. Your gluteus maximus muscles should be firm (not tight) while singing. You should feel a slight lifting up from the very bottom of these muscles.** In general, you should feel these muscles firmed in a forward direction. Some think of using the buttocks to rotate the pelvic area forward as would a ballet dancer. The American soprano Eileen Farrell, who sang with such elegant artistry, was nevertheless of base Irish stock (as I am). In her studio, she used to say to a student, "Honey, pretend you have a quarter tucked in between your butt cheeks. Now, while you're singing, don't let that quarter fall."

6. **Use the spine to hold you up.** Clearly, your spine, legs, and buttocks are always working to hold you up while you are standing, but you must be aware of them and how you use them for correct singing. **Moreover, you must use them well, because some other muscles and bones you may have been using should not be called into play. Stand tall. Elongate**

yourself. Stretch your spine upward a bit. Feel a slight bow in your back, with the inside of the curve on the back side. Your entire length, in fact, should have the slight curve of ye olde English longbow, the curve being in precisely the same direction it is when such a bow is employed. This type of curve is called *convex*.

7. Keep the chest elevated. This is an instruction that people often misunderstand. **Do not draw your chest upward or thrust it out.** Merely maintain a "proud" or military parade position, with no tensing or straining. One of my teachers spoke of imagining a string from the chin lifting the sternum up.

8. **Relax the shoulders low. Together with the chest position, you should find in looking in the mirror that your upper body has the same shape as the top of a wire coat hanger.** In fact, you should have the general feeling of a heavy winter coat hanging in a closet. A coat can never hunch up off the hanger, and neither should you ever abandon this stance. **Be sure your shoulders rotate slightly behind the upper chest muscles, helping to keep the chest in its "proud" position.**

9. **Balance the head on the neck, neither craning forward nor pulling back. Do not tilt your head to one side or the other.**

10. **Focus the eyes on the horizon or an imagined horizon, so that you do not tilt the head down. This is important when looking at music, such as on a stand. When doing so, move the stand up or look down over the tops of your cheeks at the music rather than lower your chin.**

11. **Arms hang at the sides. You should feel the arms relaxed out of their sockets. Even when gesturing, the arms and hands should be relaxed.** Imagine carrying two heavy suitcases.

Overall, you may have the sensation with good stance that you are like one of those figureheads on the bowsprit of an old sailing frigate, poised forward. My first teacher, Harry Roger Naylor, said that the professional singer's stance makes her or him feel like a thoroughbred racehorse waiting to get out of the race stalls. Good posture imbues a healthy feeling.

The stance described here is an optimal condition that should be pursued whenever possible, simply because it tends to produce the best vocal results. Naturally, if you find yourself sitting in a choir or acting in a musical or opera in which you are expected to sing seated, kneeling, or lying down, you cannot maintain this stance. Women who find themselves playing Mimi in *La Bohème* not only have to sing their last music lying down, but must convince the audience that they are dying of consumption while elegantly singing! Such performances are possible because once the elements of balance have been mastered standing, they can be transferred to other positions.

OTHER CONSIDERATIONS CONCERNING STANCE

WISDOM FROM THE OLD MASTERS

Here is what the very renowned bel canto singer and teacher Pietro Francesco Tosi writes: "He [the master] should always make the scholar sing standing, that the Voice may have all its organization free. Let him take care, whilst he sings, that he get a graceful posture, and make an agreeable Appearance" (Duey 1951, 61). You will find Mr. Duey's name appearing often in these pages. He collected, organized, and assessed singing maxims, as I do. His were of the earliest era in Western civilization. Refer to notes on him under his bibliographic citation in the back of the book.

The equally celebrated singing teacher Giovanni Battista Mancini, whose book on singing was admired and widely sold in the bel canto era, wrote:

> As for myself I always acted with my pupils like a dancing master. I used to call my pupils one by one in front of me and after having placed him in the right position, "Son," I would say, "Look, observe, ... raise your head ... don't lean forward ... nor backwards ... but straight and natural." In that position your vocal organs remain relaxed and flexible, because if you lean your head forward it [the neck] will suddenly become tense; also if the head is leaned backward. (Duey 1951, 63)

Note that Mancini is talking about the neck and head, and not the legs and hips. Mancini also stressed the need for an elevated chest.

Manfredini, another well-known teacher of this period, wrote:

> When singing, one should always hold one's head firm and straight; neither should one make any unbefitting motions with one's shoulders, arms, or any other part of one's body; on the contrary, one should hold oneself in a noble posture, and sing while standing in order that the voice might come out more easily, particularly when

studying and when one must make an effort and is anxious to be successful in being heard. (Duey 1951, 64)

My guess is that Manfredini's "noble posture" means to carry the chest high and to stand tall. He is smart enough to understand that when a singer is acting, this position must sometimes be sacrificed, so he emphasizes that the habit should be well instilled while studying.

The venerable Manuel Garcia wrote: "The body must be straight, well planted on the feet, and without any other support; the shoulders well back, the head erect, the expression of the face calm" (1847 and 1872, 12).

Antoine Bailleux (d. 1791) observed: "One should, standing or seated, maintain a graceful posture, with the body erect and head lifted without affectation. It is not necessary to gesticulate while singing nor to make grimaces with the mouth, the eyes, and forehead" (Duey 1951, 69).

Even though in the preceding paragraphs I have quoted some of the oldest sources, rest assured that these maxims are preached right through to the present day.

DIAGNOSTICS

QUESTION: I have always understood that nothing good gets accomplished by tensing up. Shouldn't we simply strive to relax our bodies while singing?
ANSWER: My teacher Roger Naylor asked the question "What would a violin string sound like if it was relaxed?" There needs to be a dynamic tension in singing, one that is based on position much more than effort. The basis for good singing begins with establishing a position and balance among the involved elements of the body, which means practically every part. The tightrope walker doesn't get from one side of the wire to the other over the abyss by being relaxed but by maintaining perfect dynamic balance.

CONCERN: Is there such a thing as bowing your spine too much forward to get a good singing position?
ANSWER: Absolutely. The ancient Greeks, who established the bases for our current Western civilization, had a saying carved into the stone pediment of their most sacred temple at Delphi: *Do nothing in excess.* We should all live by this principle. Just as someone has written, "The difference between a hobby and a mania is often about one dollar and one hour," even a little too much drawing your chest upward or thrusting your hips forward will produce unnecessary strain. Study and practice singing easily.

QUESTION: Can I put my hand on the piano when singing, or should I leave both hands at my sides?
ANSWER: If you can place one hand lightly and easily on the piano, there is no problem here. Many artists do. However, don't clutch it as a drowning man would a life preserver.

QUESTION: Holding sheet music up always seems to make it harder for me to sing freely than when I sing from memory.
ANSWER: That is because the act of holding up anything for a length of time begins to produce upper-body tension. If given a choice, set the music on a music stand, or else memorize it.

OBSERVATION: My teacher told me to always look toward the horizon or an imagined horizon while I sing. Is this correct?
ANSWER: As a general rule, it is a good one. It is also boring to the audience. It is probably best to look around and make eye contact with all your audience over the period of a song. However, setting your eyes on the horizon guides you toward keeping your head in the most free position.

QUESTION: Will not a flat back work as well as one slightly curving forward?
ANSWER: I believe the important point here is not to allow the spine to slump so that the chest collapses and the diaphragm cannot descend. An esteemed colleague and magnificent coloratura soprano, Dr. Clarissa Davis, prefers a ballet dancer's modified third position. She works for a flat back, especially when singing high notes.

CHAPTER 2

Breathing / The Torso

A virtuoso of the breath is nearest to the virtuoso of singing.
— OLD ITALIAN SCHOOL

He who knows how to breathe knows how to sing.
— MARIA CELLONI

He who breathes properly sings properly.
— PACCHIAROTTI

The art of singing is the school of respiration.
— OLD ITALIAN SCHOOL

IF YOU HAVE CONSULTED OTHER BOOKS ON SINGING, you may have seen that parallel chapters to this one are called by the fancier name *Respiration*. Nonetheless, the section on breathing will either be the first or second in every book on singing. **Breathing, is, in fact, the single most important controllable element in good singing.**

In the early 1900s, G. B. Lamperti was one of the most widely read writers on singing. He wrote: "We think it advisable, at first, to attempt exercises in breathing, and later in tone-attack, only under the teacher's personal supervision; for just at this stage much harm may be done which is hard to undo afterwards. Reason: Breath-control is the foundation of all vocal study" (1905, 9).

William Shakespeare (not the bard but a wise singing teacher with the same name) writes: "The pupil is often directed to *breathe naturally.* Now, a singer's respiration, like any other feat of strength, should be apparently natural—all signs of effort must be concealed—but in reality his respiration is *a vast extension of the ordinary breath-taking;* otherwise he would take in so small a quantity of air that with it he could sing only the very shortest phrases, and these without effect, for they would be wanting in intensity" (1898, 9).

To continue the automobile analogy from Chapter 1, you can have a workable car with a poorly made chassis, but it won't go anywhere without the engine. Breathing is the engine of singing, and how one breathes totally affects tonal quality and musicianship. Although a singer may breathe perfectly and still not sing perfectly, there is no way one can breathe poorly and sing well.

A widely accepted definition of *singing* is "extended speech on pitches." The word *extended* is at the crux of breathing in singing, although breathing affects much more, as we shall see. To live, we simply need to inhale and exhale, or, stated more scientifically, inspire and expire. This process exchanges oxygen for carbon dioxide. We do it unconsciously, although we can consciously control it. To sustain life, all we need to do is expand our lungs to create a vacuum that draws in air, and then let them deflate, slowly or quickly.

In singing, we use the lungs as a player does the bagpipes, filling the bag and doling out the air. With our instrument, the air serves to vibrate the vocal cords. Therefore, we need to hold breath back for at least as long as each required musical phrase. The holding element is the key: where and how it is done to last a long time, to make beautiful tones, and to avoid injury to the delicate singing mechanism.

In breathing to live, we have two steps: breathe in; breathe out. In breathing to sing, we have three steps: let the breath in; resist; parcel the breath out. These words are carefully chosen. What follows are the three steps in detail, and the reasons I have chosen precisely these words.

STEP 1: LET THE BREATH IN

On the intake, singing breath should be "let in" and not "taken in." Although we are unaware of it except when the wind blows, we are surrounded by and at the bottom of a vast sea of atmosphere, much of which consists of the oxygen we need to live. In fact, this sea is so deep that at sea level the pressure of all those molecules exerts a force of 14.2 pounds per square inch in every direction. We're used to it, so we don't feel it. This pressure is a very good thing for singing, because it allows us to let air come in rather than labor to draw it in.

There is a saying: "Nature abhors a vacuum." When you open a pickle jar or any other sealed food jar that has been vacuum packed, you know instantly that there is no air inside. The moment the seal is broken, a hissing occurs, telling you that the air is fighting its way in at high speed, acting under the pressure I discussed in the previous paragraph. Likewise, when you make space in your evacuated lungs, the air will automatically find its way in, provided you have open nostrils and/or an open mouth.

But why should we let air in rather than take it in? Wouldn't taking it in be quicker and get us a larger breath? No. As quickly as the lungs are expanded, the air will find its way in. *Letting* is far less taxing than *making* or *taking*. And, depending on how the breath is taken, many people actually get far less air inside when taking a breath, and they will create a tense throat in the bargain.

CLAVICULAR BREATHING

The lungs together are roughly shaped like a traffic cone or Native American teepee. I would like to offer also the analogy of a capital *A* as an equilateral triangle. Those who work at breathing, or "take breath," often lift their shoulder blades (those movable bones two-thirds of the way up your back that are our parallel to chicken wings). They help this upward process by

FIGURE 2

Front view of lungs, rib cage, and diaphragm (heavy line and dotted line)

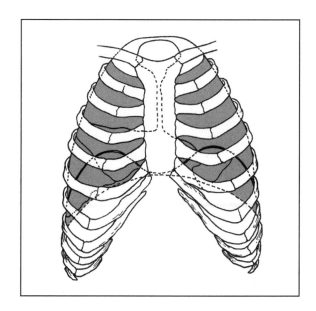

tightening their stomach muscles while shortening their rib muscles and expanding the ribs. This effort lifts the two bones at the top front of the chest between the neck and shoulders called the *clavicles* and is known as *clavicular breathing*. It is also called *shallow breathing*. It is what we do when fighting for a breath and is, unfortunately, the wrong way to get extra air. This breathing fills only the top section of the capital *A*. Study the side anatomical drawing (Figure 1) of the human torso found in the previous chapter, "Stance." Then look at Figure 2, in this chapter, a diagram taken from Shakespeare. The shaded area represents the lungs.

You will see that the lungs extend down much lower than most people believe. In fact, they very much align with the extent of the rib cage that protects both them and the heart. This means that they extend farther down in the back than in the front. You can feel in the center of your chest the bottom of the sternum (breastbone), known as the *xiphoid process* (below which the Heimlich maneuver is accomplished). Spreading your fingers down and outward from here to the sides, however, you can feel the free-floating ribs below this. They are so-called precisely because they are not rigidly attached to the front of the rib cage and so can expand much more freely.

According to the influential mid-twentieth-century singing teacher Cornelius Reid,

> Two important reasons make clavicular breathing useless as a practical technique. First of these is that by raising the chest and lifting the shoulders the muscles of the neck are brought into tension. This constitutes an unnecessary involvement and the tension of the neck muscles soon spreads until the entire upper portion of the anatomy becomes rigidly inflexible. All sense of tonal 'support,' body poise and control is speedily lost and, wanting this, the voice 'grips' instead of 'holds' and the technique gradually becomes throaty.
>
> The lesser penalty for singing with the high chest position is that only a partial inspiration can be completed. As the diaphragm is dome-shaped, the act of drawing the diaphragm upward and raising the chest means that only a fraction of its capacity for storing energy is utilized. (1950, 147–148)

Shakespeare advises:

> The first aim of the student must be to fill his lungs with air while keeping the throat loose and wide open, *and to reject altogether the habit of consciously raising the upper part of the chest.* This vicious

method enables us to breathe quickly and vigorously, but at the same time with much apparent and painful embarrassment at the throat and face, as though we were suffering from asthma or bronchitis." (1898, 15)

Note that Shakespeare does not say it will allow deep breathing.

DIAPHRAGMATIC AND INTERCOSTAL BREATHING

Remember that, as we are creatures who stand upright, our sensory organs are oriented to the front of our bodies for the benefits of binocular vision and stereophonic hearing. We very seldom think of our backs unless we have back injuries. Nevertheless, in breathing, much can and should happen in the sides and across the back around the rib area.

Make no mistake: even clavicular breathers use some low rib breathing, and their diaphragms descend and flatten somewhat. The issues of how much and by means of which muscles this is accomplished are vitally important.

Figures 3 and 4 show the correct muscles used for inspiration. (Figure 3 is a front view; Figure 4 is a back view.)

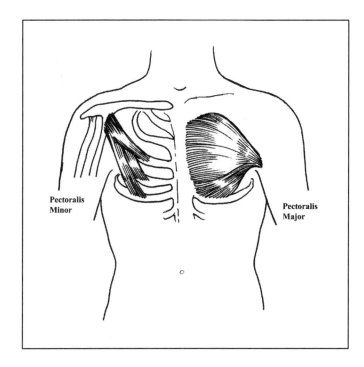

Pectoralis
Minor

Pectoralis
Major

FIGURE 3

Muscles of inspiration, anterior

15

FIGURE 4

Muscles of inspiration, posterior

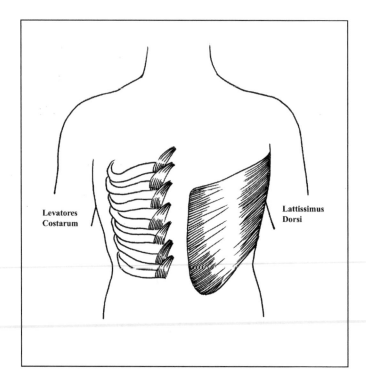

Levatores Costarum

Lattissimus Dorsi

The muscles shown in Figures 3 and 4 are all exterior muscles. All-important for breathing is a great sheath of muscle that extends across roughly the center inside your torso and that is pierced only by the big vein and artery supplying blood to and from the lower part of your body and by the esophagus leading from mouth to stomach. If this set of muscles is damaged or paralyzed, you will die from lack of oxygen. It needs to contract for the inspiration process. This is the diaphragm, shown in Figures 5 and 6.

When the diaphragm is at rest and you are in a standing position, it is shaped like an inverted bowl. It contracts to enable you to inhale. The action of the exterior muscles and ribs assists to draw it down to a flatter shape (see Figure 1). This pulls down and opens the lungs with it. The diaphragm is anchored to ribs all around. The muscles outside the ribs, beginning near the sternum and ending at the spine, contract or shorten, thus drawing the ribs out and creating a bit of space between each rib. At the same time, they lower the diaphragm. When the lower ribs and diaphragm are more fully used, this is called *diaphragmatic and intercostal breathing. Intercostal* simply means "between the ribs." This term is used because the spaces between the ribs expand and separate during inspiration (outward, upward, downward, forward, backward). Now, if the lungs are compared to an equilateral triangle divided like an *A,* the part of the *A* below the crossbar is effectively used. A student of geometry will know that this represents three triangles each the area of the top one. Thus, a great deal more air is admitted into the lungs.

In his 1898 book, Shakespeare writes, *"For singing purposes diaphragmatic breathing must be combined with rib breathing....* The inspiration, therefore, most suitable for a singer is effected by rib-raising, combined with the moderate descent of the diaphragm. This combined action is the most powerful inspiratory effort possible" (13). When reading this, be aware that he has preached lowering the diaphragm to a nearly flat position and then expanding more, so that the chest rises from extended ribs. This is not breathing up. Shakespeare goes on to say that another group of muscles pulls the ribs downward and outward. In brief, the ribs are extended in all directions while the diaphragm is lowered as flat as possible. This is not a forceful or tensing action and can barely be perceived by an outside observer.

Some students are helped by imagining a blacksmith's hand bellows. The narrow tube where the air emerges parallels our neck and windpipe. The

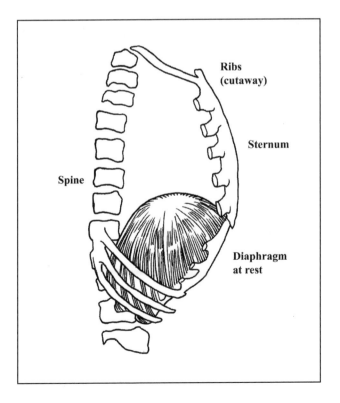

FIGURE 5

Right side cutaway view of diaphragm

Ribs
(cutaway)

Sternum

Spine

Diaphragm
at rest

FIGURE 6

The diaphragm viewed from below

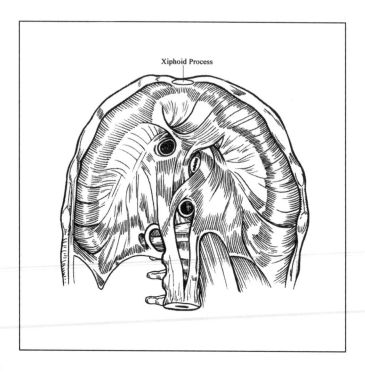

Xiphoid Process

pleated, expandable area mimics the lungs and rib cage. The place where the work is done is at the opposite end from the neck, and the bellows handles equate with the free-floating lowest ribs. Around this part of our body is where we do the vast majority of the work for both letting in and letting out breath.

We began with stance because stance greatly affects breathing. If we use the feet, legs, buttocks, and spine for support, not tensely but in balance, we have the luxury of not having to use so firmly the many muscles around our abdominal area. Why shouldn't we use these muscles to hold ourselves up and draw in breath? Because when we contract them, we compress the stomach, liver, pancreas, spleen, gall bladder, small and large intestines, and other soft organs so that they become compact. They become so tight that they impede the downward movement of the diaphragm directly above. We can't let in a large breath.

D. A. Clippinger, around whose teaching a method was formed, became popular because of correct observations such as, "When the full breath is taken the ribs move outward, upward, and forward. This enlarges the box in which the lungs are located. The lungs, which are partly compressed, follow the receding walls and a vacuum is created which outside air rushes in to fill. Air is not forced into the lungs" (1932, 6).

A much-celebrated German singing teacher was Emma Seiler, who recorded her thoughts in *The Voice in Singing*. She wrote,

> According to the Old Italian method ... the pupil ... was taught to fill his lungs more and more. But this was to be done, as much as possible, imperceptibly, noiselessly, slowly, and soon enough for him to be able properly to control the quiet breathing in the beginning of a song. Only the sides of the body were in so doing to expand, and breathing with raised chest was allowed only in exceptional cases, as where long passages were to be sung with special passion. (1900, 12)

I assume that Seiler meant in her last quoted sentence that the singer was to overfill the lungs so that the chest rising could be felt. She did not recommend clavicular breathing.

What should you feel when you let in a breath? Because the low, abdominal muscles of the front and side torso aren't impeding expansion, you should feel that letting in breath is quite easy. You will first feel the air intake from the lowering diaphragm, and then feel the ribs separate slightly. The highest pairs of ribs will lift very little, but with a full inspiration you can definitely feel this lift, as if being buoyed up. The majority of ribs are attached to the spine in the back and the breastbone (sternum) in the front, so they can't move far. The lower ribs are felt slightly descending even as they expand. The diaphragm has flattened and descended, although you can't feel it per se. However, you will feel the gentle downward pressure of it pushing all the soft organs, such as the stomach, intestines, and liver, down and out. Avoid tummy tightening during lower rib expansion.

Because of deep breathing, some people swear that their lungs go right down to their belt line. This is not true, but there is a bit of expansion all around the belt line nonetheless, because the soft organs are pushed (or compressed from above) outward. Naturally, if one is standing with firm legs and buttocks, the pelvic cavity of bone isn't going anywhere. The organs can be pushed down into it only so much. They soon begin to spill over the top of the pelvis, creating a sensation similar to the lung expansion directly above it.

You must not tighten the stomach muscles while letting in breath. Especially for young men, the notion of relaxing the stomach muscles is not welcome. They work diligently to maintain attractive, flat stomachs and what is called the "washboard" or "six-pack" look. This cannot be a goal in inspiration. Precisely these muscles must be relaxed and not called into play yet.

Think about breathing all around the chest and midsection and not merely in the front. The more the inhaling effort is distributed, the better. This is called *generalizing the effort* rather than localizing effort. Much better results occur when a singer thinks about using the full capabilities of the lungs.

Stella Owsley, who was a celebrated singer and teacher in Texas, wrote in her *Helpful Hints to Singers:*

> Now for a slow breathing exercise. Let us think of the thoracic cavity as a bag. When a paper bag or sack is filled with air it first expands at the back or bottom. So let us be conscious first of expansion in back rather than front of the thoracic cavity or chest. (We have quoted from Gray's *Anatomy* that the thoracic cavity is much deeper behind than in front.) This expansion can be felt wider about the shoulder blades and upper back [I believe she means expansion as a consequence of action below this point and not from local effort. — BJM] Some advocate that the only hold a singer can exercise is in the back directly under the scapula (shoulder blade). (1937, 31)

Regarding Owsley's last sentence, the middle-lower back muscles are certainly the ones that I and several singing colleagues "set in place" when singing high notes.

A suggestion I make to help relieve the common mistake of tightening stomach muscles in inhaling is to imagine that one has just committed hari-kari (ritual disembowelment, which is actually called *seppuku* in Japanese), cutting the torso so that the muscles can't be called into play. Another image is to think of the four sets of muscles between the sternum and the tops of the thighs as a giant earthmover scoop shovel that has just opened to drop its great load of dirt into a dump truck.

A third image I give is to think of the elegant film dancer Fred Astaire in his formal tails. The white part of his outfit — the tie, shirt, and vest — must be relaxed upon inspiration. The black parts, the swallowtail coat and trousers, are used either for inspiration or stance.

Edmund Myer, the foremost apostle of the pressure and resistance theory, which we will soon discuss, declares that "The diaphragm must press down and out, thus expanding the entire body at the waist; front, sides, and back. At the same moment, the abdomen must expand, and the chest must fill and slightly expand. This is deep inflation, and is but the work of an instant" (1891, 23).

The more a singer concentrates on expanding the lower ribs on the sides and around the back, the more the diaphragm will be aided in descending, and the greater the resulting inflow of air. The Old Masters knew by observation that the excellent singers breathed calmly, nearly imperceptibly, and with no noise. Bovicelli objects to audible breathing, "making more noise with the drawing of the breath than with the voice" (Duey 1951, 39).

HOW DO I KNOW THIS REALLY WORKS?

The Italian superstar tenor Luciano Pavarotti has the answer. He says (I paraphrase), "You want to know how to breathe to sing correctly? Do as a baby does. Don't hold your stomach in but let it rise and fall. We have all seen babies on their backs, with their little bellies going up and down. They have the tiniest, most unformed lungs, and yet they can scream for hours so loudly that we will give them whatever they want. And yet they never grow hoarse. Have you ever heard a hoarse baby?"

It is my opinion that we are born breathing well, but we lose this habit by observing those around us doing it poorly. You may say to yourself, "I have never watched anyone to learn how to breathe." And yet if you think about it, your stock phrases, your speaking accent, your facial expressions, the subtlest elements of your life have all been assimilated unconsciously. Unfortunately, this is also true of bad breathing.

STEP 2: SET TO RESIST

Having let in a large, well-coordinated breath through the nose and mouth doesn't do much good if, on the first note, most of it goes whooshing out. **Instinctively, we all know that we must hold back the flow of air in order to last until the end of the vocal phrase. How we accomplish this, however, makes the greatest difference in the production of tone.**

This second step is the extra one for singing that we do not need for life. Put most simply, it **is a pact you make with yourself that wherever your ribs and diaphragm have expanded to, you will not let them collapse or spring back into a relaxed condition until you have finished using that breath. It is as simple as turning the lock on a closed door.**

I will stress yet again that **this is not hard work. No great tension is necessary.** This action is called *resistance*. Some call it *balance*. It involves the diaphragm dynamically tense like the head of a kettle drum or tympanum and the ribs helping to keep it taut, as do the screws around the outside of the drum. These are necessary to counter the pressure from below that is used for expiration. This results in highly controlled husbanding and feeding out of air.

Edmund J. Myer writes:

Let it not be supposed that any one can sing with magnificent power, beauty, and dramatic force without effort. On the other hand, the entire body, mind and soul are in action, and yet to the singer, and to the listener, all effort is lost sight of in the graceful, natural manner in which it is done, and in the magnificent result.

To reach this point one must master all mechanical movements, must make them a part of oneself; must so train and strengthen the muscles which produce voice that, in time, that which was difficult becomes easy, because automatic. (1891, 16)

Lamperti is credited with saying, "All there is in singing is in the breathing, and all there is in breathing is in the diaphragm." He also writes: "The act of tone-production is in 'contrary motion' to that of breath-taking: the pull of the diaphragm goes parallel with the inspiration [that is, downward], whereas the push of the abdominal muscles is felt to oppose it (observe the movement of the abdominal walls), although both stand in causal conjunction. The breath-pressure increases regularly as the pitch in the tone rises. With insufficient pressure, the tone lacks in steadiness (*appoggio;* that is, the steady air-pressure on the vocal cords during tone-production). Higher breath-pressure presupposes deeper inspiration. Each and every tone must have steady support!" (1905, 9).

According to Shakespeare, "The sensation accompanying a right breath-control is that of restraining, balancing, and regulating the inspiratory muscles; they refuse to allow the expiratory muscles to press out the breath except as the will of the singer determines. It seems to the good singer as though the breath, while being vigorously pressed out, *still remains inside the body.* **The breath is felt now to be *under* the note; that is to say, the control of the breath is under the note, which, when sounding fully, may be said to be *on the breath*"** (1898, 20). This is a very important concept and is generally understood fully by a singer only after she or he has begun to balance diaphragmatic resistance above abdominal pressure.

Clippinger writes,

When the lungs are full there is an enormous contracting power at work in the effort to get back to a condition of rest. It is at this point that the difficulty in controlling and economizing the breath manifests itself. Something must be opposed to the pressure from without and the diaphragm alone can successfully accomplish it. If the diaphragm remains vitalized it will successfully resist the pressure from without and enable the singer to keep the breath under control. (1932, 8)

I disagree with Clippinger's "diaphragm alone" theory. The outside muscles attached to the ribs must be used in concert with the diaphragm. Also, when he speaks of the "pressure from without," it seems as if he means the air pressure outside the body. This exists, but we must be much more aware of and able to counter the expiratory pressure arising from the muscles of the abdomen. Toward this end, the diaphragm alone without the aid of the rib muscles can't do the job.

Edmund J. Myer's book *Vocal Reinforcement: A Practical Study,* as one might expect, fixates on the need for finding the means to reinforce the breath pressure to produce smooth, powerful tones. In his introduction Myer writes, "A right training of the voice may be said to be a study of reinforcement" (1891, 11).

Henderson reminds us of how we must use the correct muscles to "set": "In the practice of deep breathing, after the lungs have been filled the air should be retained for two or three seconds before exhalation [only in breathing exercises]. This retention is not to be accomplished by closing the vent in the larynx.... The breath must be retained simply by the action of the diaphragm and rib muscles. The throat must be kept lax and open" (1906, 29–30). I assume that Henderson means by *vent* the epiglottis just above the voice box, which is used in swallowing and can shut off the outflow of air.

LET IN, SET, SPIN
When I teach students, I remind them of the required three-part breathing with the words "Let in, set, spin." *Set* may give you the image of cement setting. For the length of that breath, it is quite like that.

STEP 3: PARCEL THE BREATH OUT

When I was a Boy Scout, they had a merit badge called "Animal Husbandry," which I thought was a strange phrase. Then I learned that *to husband* means "to take good care of, to conserve, and to manage economically." Accomplished singers husband their breaths on the way out. This is different than mere expiration, in which case it doesn't matter how quickly you exhale.

In this third part of the singer's breath, you **gently recruit** the four powerful sets of muscles across your midsection from your sternum to your groin. These are the muscles shown in Figures 7 and 8. Go back to the drawings of

FIGURE 7

Central muscles of expiration, rectus and transverse abdominus (transverse underlies and runs completely across)

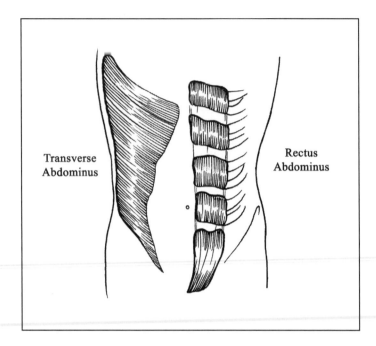

Transverse Abdominus

Rectus Abdominus

FIGURE 8

Side muscles of expiration, external and internal obliques

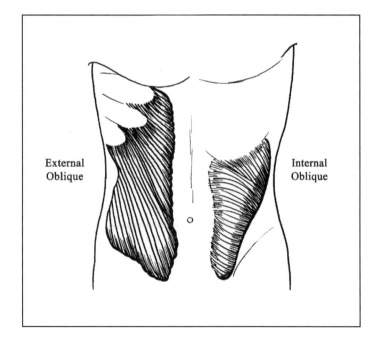

External Oblique

Internal Oblique

the muscles of inspiration, Figures 3 and 4, and note that none of the muscles around the stomach is indicated for inspiration.

In looking at the drawings in Figures 7 and 8, you will see that the central and side muscles of expiration constitute huge masses of muscle. They are large and powerful enough to bring you upright when lying flat on the floor to execute sit-ups and crunches. When I was twelve, I had to have my appendix removed. These muscles were cut on the right side, and I couldn't believe how helpless I was to move for more than a week, even at that limber age.

Although the human body is a marvel of creation, evolution, or both, depending on your beliefs, the mechanism of inhalation is not entirely efficient, in that the lungs are expanded by contraction from the outside rather than pushed out from the inside by some other process. Consequently, it is easy to let them go when they are countered by the contraction of the very efficient sets of muscles of the abdominal area. It's basically a two-against-one situation. Therefore, **when exhaling, one must not push hard in any one place with the abdominal muscles. It is further recommended that at the beginning of the phrase, one begin pressing upward gently from the area where the torso joins the legs.** This is a simple matter of leverage. Think why we place a door handle or knob on the side of the door opposite the hinges. If we were to place the handle near the hinges, we would have much less mechanical advantage. It is much easier to control gentle and steadily sustained exhalation from lower than from higher. Moreover, you will find that if you immediately begin to press out the air from under the breastbone, you will quickly exhaust your control and cannot press in any more. You can press higher if you start low, but pressing high first and then seeking later to use your low muscles will not work.

J. Van Broekhoven agrees with this theory and succinctly states, "Breath control, which comprehends *inhalation, retention* and *expulsion* of the breath, can be gained only by individual experience and practice." He further says, "*Retention* of the breath is rarely mentioned by vocal teachers, and yet it is of the greatest importance in singing to be able to retain for a long time the breath in the lungs. Breath retaining should therefore be practiced aside from singing, for the purpose of strengthening the retaining muscles of the chest, and enabling the singer to control his breath with ease" (1908, 19–20). This is the "set," the middle of the three steps.

Myer writes that "A correct singing tone is not the result of breath in escape, but of breath imprisoned, compressed and controlled in exit" (1891, 41). Among the most vivid and compelling images regarding this business of resistance against pressure also comes from Myer: "It is the quantity of steam that cannot escape that makes the train go; it is the quantity of gas that cannot get out that makes the balloon ascend; it is the quantity of wind that cannot pass through a sail that propels the ship; and it is the quantity of breath that cannot escape that makes us sing" (42).

The Old Italian Masters said, *"We do not sing with the breath; we sing on the breath."* **They intended that the tone actually seems like a little boat, buoyed up by a constant, pressurized column of air. No air is to escape around the tone, causing extraneous noise like chiff from an organ pipe.**

Perhaps the most famous, most widely translated (from German), and most used vocal training book by a singer was written by Lilli Lehmann. In English, its title is *How to Sing*. Lehmann sums up her long investigation as a pupil into the art of breathing as follows:

> Finally I abandoned all superfluous drawing in of the abdomen and diaphragm, inhaled but little, and began to pay special attention to emitting the smallest possible amount of breath, which I found very serviceable.
>
> I draw in the diaphragm and my abdomen just a little, only to relax it immediately [This is a different, more complicated technique than I preach, but I have seen it done successfully on the operatic stage—BJM]. I raise the chest, distend the upper ribs, and support them with the lower ones like pillars under them. In this manner I prepare the form for my singing, the supply chamber for the breath. …At the same time I raise my palate high toward the nose and prevent the escape of breath through the nose. (1924, 19)

Cornelius Reid writes, "Tension evenly balanced and maintained as in a correct manner of breathing leads to a precision of attack, i.e. the instantaneous sound of a definite pitch, vowel and intensity, otherwise impossible. All noise, breathiness and other impurities are simultaneously eliminated" (1950, 153).

OTHER CONSIDERATIONS CONCERNING BREATHING

THE OLDER SINGER AND BREATHING

Those singers fifty years of age or older should be aware that from approximately that point onward, the lungs begin to lose their elasticity. It is not uncommon to have lost 20 percent of lung capacity by age sixty. Consequently, phrasing must be adjusted and more breaths let in.

BREATHING EXERCISES

A very simple breathing exercise was offered by Farinelli, the greatest castrato singer of the eighteenth century, as his Great Exercise: "Sip the breath slowly and steadily through the smallest possible opening of the lips; hold it a few counts, then exhale very slowly and steadily through the smallest possible opening of the lips" (Duey 1951, 85).

This technique has several good things going for it: the mouth should be used as part of the inspiration (but not the only part); breathing should be in three parts (but he doesn't speak of resistance); exhaling slowly shows the student that the singing breath should be husbanded.

Here is a more complete and productive exercise for mastering three-part breathing:

1. Take the position described in Chapter 1, "Stance."
2. Relax your arms out of their shoulder sockets.
3. Rotate your wrists outward so that you can see them, and then look back up to the horizon.
4. On a slow mental count from one to five, pivot your hands outward and slightly upward in a natural curve, at the same time expanding all of the rib cage, particularly the lower and back parts. The wrists act as a more visible and perceptible partner in helping to guide the ribs out and the diaphragm down. Be sure the shoulders remain low.
5. On a slow mental count of five, hold the ribs in place and refuse to let the chest collapse. There should be no tension.
6. Maintaining this chest position, on a slowly spoken count of five, let out a small but steady flow of breath, with the impulse and control from the lowest abdominal muscles. Allow the wrists to slowly descend and come back to the sides.
7. Relax the entire torso for a moment.
8. Repeat the exercise ten times.

Shakespeare recommends a similar exercise but asks the student to let the breath in and out rapidly, as in dog pants (1898, 16).

I cannot stress too much that this exercise is not hard work. Nor should any aspect of singing be strenuous. My first teacher, Roger Naylor, used to tell me that "singing is 90 percent mental and only 10 percent physical." He also said, "Effort in singing should be so balanced and free from restraint that it is not apparent." Think first, understand, assimilate, imagine. Then easily attempt to put your thinking into action.

Once you have mastered the exercise, begin to do it without use of the arms and wrists. This very important exercise can be done at virtually any time. For example, when you inevitably get into the slowest line at the store or post office, you can practice. You can also practice breathing while waiting in the doctor's office or sitting on a bus or airplane, although the sitting position is not as advantageous. Simply be sure you are sitting up straight, with your buttocks and spine holding you up.

ANOTHER ANGLE ON THE BREATHING EXERCISE

Some people experience quicker results lying with their backs flat on a hard floor, such as a wooden one, and their knees slightly bent with their legs partway drawn up. Their arms are relaxed at their sides, palms down, and their eyes look straight up. Again, the key is to relax the abdominal muscles and not bring them into play. Because the floor will not give, you will find your belly rising as a baby's would if the diaphragm is being brought into proper action. This is from organs pushing out as the diaphragm flattens and not from using the abdominal muscles.

Here is how the teacher Behnke recommends the exercise be done: "Divest yourself of any article of clothing which at all interfere with the freedom of the waist. Lie down on your back. Place one hand lightly on the abdomen and the other upon the lower ribs. Inhale, through the nostrils, slowly, deeply, and evenly, without interruption, or jerking. If this is done properly the abdomen will, gradually and without any trembling movement, increase in size, and the lower ribs will expand sideways, while the upper part of the chest and the collar bones remain undisturbed" (189?, 106).

I personally do not think that one should place hands anywhere but at the sides on the floor after the first few trials. Otherwise, these "locating" placements begin to form a crutch habit. Also, I believe that the upper part of the chest also rises, but it does so slightly after the lower area does and in proportion to its smaller cross-section. The collarbones do not move, as he states. Letting some air in through the mouth at the same time is proper.

A FINAL EXERCISE TO COAX GOOD BREATHING POSITION

This technique was shared with me by Elizabeth Strauss, who was a fellow student at IU and is a present colleague: raise the arms straight up over the head and interlace the fingers. Now concentrate on "breathing down" and flattening the diaphragm, with your mouth slightly open. You will feel the air being drawn into the lungs. Once you have expanded, set the ribs and chest muscles. Then lower your arms to your sides. You will note how this technique compels a high chest position and a slight concave arch to your back. If you do the opposite of this exercise and let your chest collapse and your shoulders roll forward, you will find that lowering the diaphragm is almost impossible. This technique is also good because it discourages the tightening of the abdominal muscles during inspiration, which I have found to be a common problem among students.

ADDED BENEFITS OF GOOD BREATHING

You will find as you do the exercises listed above that you are feeling more generally relaxed and calm. Deep breathing is a common practice of relaxation, from health clubs to the Alexander Technique to Zen masters. When you breathe deeply, you need to breathe less often. This also relaxes you. Deep breathing is said to massage the heart in a beneficial manner, since it sits directly atop the diaphragm. Although radical oxygen molecules are not good for your body on a cellular level, extra oxygen in the bloodstream is. This surfeit of oxygen helps to clean the blood and nourish cells.

Good singers are professional breathers. The benefits are most tellingly seen in opera singers. Because of the nature of their lives, many are overweight and don't exercise enough. I also have a pet theory I can't prove—that there are so many heavy opera singers because the excess weight around their torsos prevents them from "breathing up" and from contracting their abdominal muscles. Being overweight actually compels good breathing (but doesn't guarantee it, to be sure; nor do I recommend it, since thin people such as Frank Sinatra, Lily Pons, and Celine Dion have sung extremely well). Whatever the case, the average overweight person usually dies years before the norm; overweight opera singers often live beyond the norm. One explanation may be the relaxing and nourishing effects of diaphragmatic and intercostal breathing.

HOW THE GOOD BREATH COMES OUT: "FILAR IL SUONO"

The important Old Italian singing master adage *filar il suono* means "spin out the sound." The verb *spin* is an excellent one for your imagination, because a proper singing breath is a fine current, akin to spun thread, not coarse rope. The first point of this adage is that the breath must come out continuously, like a long thread rather than bits of lint. The second is that it comes out in a thin, focused current. This is why I remind the student to "spin" when I say "Let in/set/spin."

The word *spin* may remind you of spiders. Most have the capability of making webs from spider silk. Ounce for ounce, this very thin material is stronger than steel, which proves that mass alone does not tell the story in accomplishing a task. This is particularly true regarding air and tone. Focused exhaled air, although "husbanded," is also very strong.

The great master Lamperti said, "Do not 'Hold' your tone, spin it. Hold your breath" (Brown 1931, 29).

HOW AIR MAKES TONE

Amazingly, no matter how close you get to your birthday cake, it's still hard to blow out all the candles. And yet if you stand on the far side of a quiet room and whisper to someone else, they will hear you. **A common misapprehension regarding singing is that large volumes of air must be pushed past the vocal cords and out the mouth when one wants to sing high or loudly. Such action only exhausts the breath quickly.** It also produces the condition known as *breathy tone* or *husky tone*. Remember how Marilyn Monroe talked and sang? She was not one who could sing a long phrase, and her loudness resulted from a microphone dangling just above her head or from lip synching. The air surrounding us carries the energy of air waves as medium, just as the ocean carries the energy of waves to shore. This pulsed energy acts on air molecules outside our ears and causes them to press against the eardrums. These are not the same molecules of air that came from the lungs.

Air is required for us to hear sound but not to reach from our mouths to our listeners' ears. The breath is instead required in singing to make the vocal cords vibrate. If the throat is unrestricted (what we'll later call "open"), the thinnest column of air will make the cords vibrate. What is required for high and for intense tones is that this thin column of air be under sufficient pressure.

Muckey presented a novel image to prove this fact:

> The present definitions of the voice by teachers, critics, and others show that they cannot appreciate the nature of the voice. Voice is variously defined as 'vocalized breath,' 'vibrated breath,' 'vitalized breath'.… The voice is air-waves, which like those of any other sound, travel at the rate of 1,100 feet per second or about 750 miles per hour. Breath is an air current, and air-current traveling at the rate of 750 miles per hour would destroy everything in their path. (1915, 111–112)

The Old Italian Masters checked that their pupils were not wasting unnecessary breath by two methods: if they were in a cold room (which probably happened often in centuries past), they would have the pupil step close to a mirror and sing. If the mirror fogged, too much air was being expelled. Alternately, they placed the pupil in front of a candle. If the flame flickered, the need for better breath resistance technique was indicated.

An analogy can be made between singing air and electrical current. Current has three major characteristics: voltage, amperage, and ohms. Volts measure the force, amperes the current, and ohms the resistance. Singing breath, too, depends not merely on the volume of current but also on the force behind it and the force impeding it.

PRESSURE AND RESISTANCE

All of nature seems to be diametric: dark and light, waking and sleeping, motion and rest. **Breathing to sing requires a balance of pressure and resistance. The pressure comes from the abdominal muscles during expiration; the resistance comes from setting the strong muscles of the chest, ribs, and middle back to keep the diaphragm low and taut. The greater the pressure from below, the greater the balancing resistance must become.**

The objective of this balance is that the thin stream of breath rising from the lungs past the vocal cords and eventually out the mouth will be under control. It allows the air to emerge with intensity and yet not with great capacity. When more sound (decibels) is wanted, the vocal cords vibrate with precisely the same number of vibrations (pitch), but the amplitude of their motion increases (strength/loudness). The thin column of air naturally guarantees that there will be enough air to sing long phrases.

The net effect of this pressure-versus-resistance push in two directions is near zero. Nor should it require strain or great tension. It is what is called *dynamic tension.*

One of my teachers, D. Ralph Appelman, termed this aspect of singing *the point of suspension:*

> The point of suspension is the body sensation created by a balanced pressure of the thoracic [chest] muscles of inspiration opposed by the abdominal muscles of expiration.
>
> Such a state of balanced suspension may be illustrated by pressing the palms of the hands together, and increasing the pressure of each hand against the other. The hands do not move because the pressures exerted are equal.
>
> In singing, the driving force of the abdominal musculature often exceeds the resisting force of the thoracic muscles, and controls are lost. Ideally, the entire scale should be sung on the point of suspension where thoracic and abdominal pressures are balanced. Such a condition assures complete control of intensities as well as changes of interval. (1974, 11)

31

If the strong muscles of the torso are not used to resist the outflow of breath, another means is possible. This control, however, produces *throaty tones* and is injurious to the vocal apparatus. We will examine this in the next chapter.

BREATHE DOWN / SING UP

The higher the pitch of a tone, the greater the tension that is necessary for any set of vocal cords to produce the pitch. To get the cords to vibrate, more pressure must come from the abdominal muscles. Therefore, greater resistance must come from the muscles above to maintain a balance. As a reminder to maintain this balance, many teachers preach "Breathe down/ sing up" and "The higher we sing, the more we must resist down," or "To sing up, think down."

Myer writes, "Never breathe up and sing down. Always breathe down and sing up. This refers, of course, entirely to the movements of the body.... The direction of effort in ascending must never go with the tone, but always away from it" (1911, 72).

Lunn directs the student to "Think downward to meet the tone – in other words, reverse the direction of vital force" (1904, 13).

Lamperti writes, "The higher the tones, the deeper the breathing" (1905, 12).

THE NOSE AND MOUTH IN INHALING

For ordinary breathing, letting all air in through the nostrils is sufficient. However, the extra volume of air required for sustained singing and the short time between many vocal phrases demand that we augment the openings of the nostrils by slightly opening the mouth, as well. Otherwise, when you relax the abdominal muscles and begin to let in a full breath, this fuller method of inspiring taxes the nostrils. They are actually sucked inward by the high pressure. A moment later, we find ourselves using the stomach muscles to assist, which is precisely what we do not want to do.

The mouth should be open only about the width of the pinkie finger between the upper and lower teeth. As a general rule, about one-third to one-half of the air should be let in through the mouth and no more. The reason is that the nostrils are far better equipped for breathing. They have hairs for filtering out dust and adapted mucus membranes that warm and moisten the air. If we breathe too much by the mouth, we find ourselves with *cotton mouth,* that dry condition that eventually has our lips sticking to our teeth.

Cornelius L. Reid writes in 1950, "Another unfortunate habit of breathing sometimes employed in singing is taking the breath through the nose with the mouth tightly closed. The practice of this fanciful notion is one of the newer developments in voice-training methods and its invention probably has necessitated by the increasing prevalence since the turn of the century, of unnatural habits of tone production" (148). He gives arguments against it as being "stilted and awkward," prohibiting the "inhalation of the requisite amounts of air," and leading "to a high chest position," by which I understand that he means clavicular breathing.

The great singing teacher Manuel Garcia encouraged his pupils to keep the mouth open the right amount by placing in between their upper and lower front teeth a tiny cork such as the ones used to stopper thin test tubes. He ended the practice, however, when one of the students inhaled too forcefully, sucked the cork down the windpipe, and almost choked to death. Your pinkie or watching in a mirror will do just fine to check until you can automatically remember.

A sensation that may occur to you when you allow yourself to breathe deeply and freely is that you can actually feel the air molecules flowing into your nostrils and over your lips, as if you are trying to smell a rose.

Well-taken (let-in) breaths will never tighten the facial or neck muscles. They also will never result in an involuntary lowering of the tongue.

The Silent and Imperceptible Breath

Many teachers have noted that well-taken breaths make no noise or effort. According to Cooke, "The breath should be taken without any appearance of effort" (1828, introduction). Panofka noted, "Breathe without noise, sobs, or sighs" (1859, 7).

Shakespeare and Mackenzie tell the story of the great singer Louis Lablache watching the greater singer Rubini sing "for four minutes without being able to see him inspire" (Shakespeare 1910, 15; Mackenzie 1891, 95).

Taylor writes, "It is of the utmost importance that the inspiration in singing be absolutely noiseless. Any noise caused by the taking of the breath is a sign of throat stiffness" (1914, 33). I heartily agree with Taylor. In fact, whenever students stand out of my line of vision while I accompany them, I can tell by their throat and pharyngeal noise before they begin a phrase that they have taken a breath incorrectly. Poor inspiration, as has been said previously, tightens the throat.

A bit of imagery that may help you keep your breathing quiet and imperceptible is to imagine your torso like a heavy winter coat on a wooden hanger. It is impossible for the coat to shrug up off the hanger. Similarly, you should keep that flattened-triangle hanger position all the while you are letting in air and never allow your shoulders or shoulder blades to rise up.

WHAT THE OLD MASTERS WROTE ABOUT BREATH

The following are all found in Philip A. Duey's authoritative work *Bel Canto in Its Golden Age* (1951):

Rossetti states, "The singer must breathe easily and not with anxiety, the breath must not seem to be drawn in violently…. The breath must strike the palate fully and the voice and breath must be emitted uniformly."

Caccini (ca. 1546–1618), who wrote a famous treatise called *Nuove Musiche,* on his period's music, observed that "A man must have a command of breath to give the greater spirit to the increasing and diminishing of the voice…. Therefore let him take heed that [because of] spending much breath upon such notes, it [the breath] does not afterward fail him in such place as it is most needful."

Donati (1636) focuses on breath control when he writes that "singing from the first to the last must be done with equal breath." This can be accomplished only with a resistance equal to the pressure of exhalation.

Mancini wrote, "One must acquire through study the art to conserve, hold, save, and retake the breath with perfect ease. Without such an acquisition, no agility of any kind can be performed." If we substitute "set, spin, and let in" for these terms, we may have duplicated the so-called secrets of bel canto breath control.

WHAT THE NEW MASTERS AGREED ON

According to D. A. Clippinger in his *Fundamentals of Voice Training*:

The American Academy of Teachers of Singing on December 9th, 1925, adopted the following:

BREATHING

1. Believes in teaching the pupil how to breathe.
2. Believes that the correct practice of singing in itself tends to develop and establish the mastery of the breath.
3. Believes that the singer should stand comfortably erect, with the chest medium high, and with a feeling of flexibility and well-being.
4. Favors that method of breathing which is known scientifically as "Diaphragmatic-Costal," colloquially as "deep breathing."
5. Believes that, in inhalation the upper abdomen expands, owing to the descent of the diaphragm, and the ribs expand; in exhalation the abdomen tenses and contracts, owing to the pressure of the abdominal muscles and to the gradual ascent of the diaphragm,

and the ribs contract. Thus the greatest observable effect in both inhalation and exhalation is in front and at the sides in the region of the waist-line. (1929, 28–29)

PEARLS ON A STRING

A fairly famous teaching image that has been used for at least two centuries is that tones and the syllables associated with them should flow seamlessly from a singer like pearls on a string. The string is the thin column of uninterrupted breath that we have addressed in an earlier section of this chapter (headed: "How the Good Breath Comes Out"). This image may help singers remember to keep their breath stream moving and to sing legato, but there is also a danger in this image. It is better to imagine tones (produced in the throat) floating on the constant column of air emerging from the lungs like the bobbing boats I mentioned earlier. The breath must always stay under the tone. When unused breath emerges with the tone, it is perceived by the listener as breathy, and the sound gets clouded or, as some have described it, "wrapped in cotton." Having tone under the breath means using just enough air to make the cords vibrate for the desired pitch and intensity.

CLUES TO INCORRECT BREATHING

If you are taking in breath rather than letting it in, two clues may prove this. These are big indicators for me when watching and listening to my students. The first is that the jaw drops as the breath is taken, as if it is being dragged down. The second is that there is a faint, hollow echo with the breath intake. This is caused by the tensed walls of the pharynx as the air is drawn in. The tensing narrows the passage and of necessity speeds up the flow of the air. Both cause this telltale sound.

DIAGNOSTICS

CONCERN: What are the faults of breathing?

ANSWER: Garcia uses question-and-answer in his book, and he responds to this question thus: "The greatest are that the breathing should be scanty, hurried, noisy, or drawn in by raising the shoulders. When the air is inhaled gradually and not by jerks, it does not rebound, and is retained by the lungs without fatigue" (1894, 5).

CONCERN: My singing feels free and powerful, and I believe I use my diaphragm, but I can feel my upper chest rise when I breathe.

ANSWER: Nothing wrong with that, as long as it isn't localized and you're breathing with your entire lungs, and if your shoulders and shoulder blades don't hunch up. You will feel a slight rise of the chest, as part of the generalized letting in of breath. However, it will probably come a moment after the diaphragm is flattened. Just as a water balloon fills in the bottom first until it stretches as far as is reasonable and then fills in the top, so do the lungs tend to fill this way.

PROBLEM: When I relax my stomach muscles and breathe diaphragmatically, I feel as if I'm barely breathing.

ANSWER: This is because you are now generalizing your inspiration rather than localizing it. There is less strain on those muscles and bones you formally used. It only feels as though less air is coming in. When you have truly mastered deep breathing, you will have much more air to work with than when you felt your lungs were full.

Parenthetically, I occasionally have problems with students who, consciously or unconsciously, feel they don't have enough breath with the changed breathing style. They equate less tension with less breath. I find that they have let in a sufficient amount, but the moment before they begin to sing, they tighten their stomachs and draw up their chests a bit, sucking in the oxygen equivalent of a security blanket. This action ultimately serves to unbalance the system and to make free singing more difficult.

QUESTION: Should I take one big breath or many little breaths?

ANSWER: **An important but anonymous old maxim stated, "Let in many breaths; do not take one large breath."** This, however, depends on the demands of the music. First, you should *let in* and not *take* breath. When allowed a space of several silent seconds, you should fill your lungs slowly. You should also breathe whenever the musicality, phrasing, and syllables of the song allow. In general, several medium or even small breaths are better than one big one unless the sense of the phrasing demands it. As far as musicality is concerned, you will be less likely to lag behind your accompaniment if you let in a smaller breath. Also, for those other than the most perfect breathers, securing a large breath risks unbalancing the respiratory system. Provided each breath is let in freely and set, the more often you renew, the more secure the sound will be and the easier you will find it to supply a steady (but focused or thin) column of air.

Lilli Lehmann wrote: "At such times [as] one must sing with peculiar circumspection, and with an especially powerful stream of breath behind the tone: it is better to take breath frequently" (1924, 19).

QUESTION: What is a *catch breath?*

ANSWER: This is a singer's term for a quick half-breath that must be taken when singing phrases too long for one breath. In many cases, a half breath is sufficient to finish the phrase comfortably. In my particular understanding, a catch breath is one obtained by recruiting the lowest of the abdominal muscles in support of the normal rib muscles. You simply draw them down quickly and slightly. This, however, is a technique that should be used sparingly and only in support of good breathing once that has been mastered. Despite the speed with which this breath must be taken (here I *mean* to take in rather than let in), an extra instant is still required to set.

PROBLEM: Sometimes a phrase is so long that I find myself whooping in the next breath, which completely upsets my good breathing technique.
ANSWER: This will happen to the advancing student. The solution is that you must plan your breaths so that you are not surprised and upset. This should not be a problem. Unless you are sight-reading, singing is not like speaking off the cuff but rather like reciting a prepared speech. You must plan breaths just as you learn the pitches and the dynamics. More about this under the section "Phrasing" in Chapter 11. I also caution my students not to fall in love with the long note that so often falls at the end of a phrase. If they are singing well, the temptation is to hold it to impress themselves, the teacher, and/or an audience. What often follows is too little time to renew the breath and a whooped-in breath that has no balance.

PROBLEM: I can't think about how I'm breathing and sing artistically at the same time.
Answer: You're absolutely correct. That is why you must practice good breathing over and over, slowly and diligently, long before you perform. The most difficult task I have with students is getting them to carry over their breath technique once they have begun to sing a song. They are too intent on musicianship to remember to attach the technical aspects from the start of the session. In effect, the logical understanding of breathing that occurs in the front of the brain must slowly be transferred to the automatic (autonomic) system in the lower back of the brain. Remember the old joke about the person who wanted to know how to get to Carnegie Hall: Practice, practice, practice. There is no shortcut.

PROBLEM: I try to let go of the muscles around my stomach area, but I feel as if I can let go only so much.
ANSWER: This is common. A similar situation is the person who has been so tight in this region while drawing in (I mean exactly that) the breath that when the singer relaxes halfway, it seems so much freer by comparison that she or he thinks the job is done, only to find the throat still tense.

My suggestion is to stop thinking so locally about this letting go and coax abdominal relaxation from a different place. The lying-on-the-floor exercise helps here. Also, experimenting with creating more and more freedom in the throat area will have a pronounced, and sometimes sudden, reflex action that will allow the abdominal muscles to relax more completely. Whatever the results produced, your immediate litmus test for success is that it must be simple and easy to attain. There are no contortions or complicated acts to the breath process. Keep concentrating on the right things to do, and gradually you will find that you relax the abdomen.

Concern: I feel like my lungs go down to my belt with all the expansion. Answer: Air does not directly cause this expansion, but rather it is caused by the lowered diaphragm pushing the soft organs of the abdominal area down and out over the top edge of the pelvic cavity.

CHAPTER 3

Phonation/The Throat

DEFINITION

ACCORDING TO VICTOR ALEXANDER FIELDS,

> phonation is the act or process of generating vocal sound; it is the inception of vocal tone at its point of production in the larynx. More explicitly, phonation is the vibratory activity of the vocal cords, so as to produce pulsations sufficiently rapid to cause the sensation of tone. (1947, 98)

THE IMPORTANCE OF CORRECT PHONATION

We have learned how important the control of breath is. Now this engine must be turned into useful activity. In the case of the automobile, the turning of the cylinders and crankshaft is connected by the transmission to the wheels for movement. In the case of that part of the vocal instrument lying inside the throat, the larynx turns the energized air into sound.

Van Broekhoven writes, "The vocal tone is *produced in the larynx,* and is no longer under the control of the singer's will when it passes out of the larynx into the throat cavities, the pharynx and the mouth.... No position of the pharynx, palate, uvula, tongue or lips will improve a tone when it is poorly produced in the larynx" (1905, 8).

This is true enough when we remember that pure tone does not make intelligible sounds. All of our instrument above the larynx filters and sympathetically resonates the spectrum (or full palette) of raw tone into words of varying fullness. In cruder terms, by how freely we allow the larynx to do its work, we can color the pictures we offer our audience with either a six-hue or a sixty-four-hue box of crayons.

However, nothing we consciously do in this laryngeal portion of the singing mechanism can make it work better. If we believe that the Old Master saying "An Italian singer has no throat" is a valid aphorism, at least from the aspect of sensation, and if we accept Fields's definition, we can conclude that **the mechanics of phonation are unconscious and automatic. They should endure no local control. The less it is dwelt upon, the better.**

Since Panseron offered the first reasonable explanation of the human phonatory process in 1849, hundreds of thousands of words have been written about precisely how it takes place. In my estimation, none of it serves more purpose than satisfying your curiosity. Examining how the human larynx, unique among all living creatures, functions somewhat like a reed instrument, a string instrument, and a brass instrument will not enable you to sing better.

Figure 9 is a drawing, after Van Broekhoven, of the larynx. What you should take away after studying this drawing is simply that many muscles, ligaments, and bones are involved, and all of them are delicate when compared

FIGURE 9

The Larynx

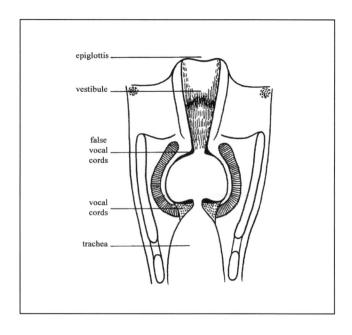

with those of the torso. Therefore, you must treat them gently and with respect if you want to sing well and for many years.

The main point to reflect on regarding phonation is that you must use the strong muscles of the torso in perfect coordination in order to have the luxury of keeping the throat open and free. The easiest place in the entire singing mechanism to hold back necessary airflow is at the throat "choke point." However, only if local constriction is not used to hold back the air from escaping can the throat create all the full, rich wavelengths necessary to produce beautiful tones in the head. Furthermore, a "tight" throat is an unhealthy one.

It is certain that the laws of acoustics apply identically to all singers with no exception, just as the law of gravity applies to everyone.

THE THROAT

The less said and thought about the throat, at least in terms of "what I must do to sing," the better. Nature has made this marvel extremely self-regulating.

The vocal cords act somewhat like the reeds in wind instruments, in that they vibrate up and down. The number of times they vibrate controls the pitch. We control the tilting of the cartilage and the tightening of muscles around the cords to vary their length and tension. Fortunately, years of trial-and-error practice have made us quite good at this with no conscious thought attached. **Our goal is to allow the throat to do its work with total freedom.**

AN ITALIAN SINGER HAS NO THROAT

The Old Italian Masters said, "An Italian singer has no throat." By this, they meant that the singers could feel no tension whatsoever in the throat area and made no conscious movements there as they sang. The throat seemed to vanish. The "proud" chest could be felt rising up; the jaw could be felt relaxing downward from the ears. But literally nothing could be felt in between. The entire inner throat seems to hang from the jaw like a sock from a clothesline. The dimple at its base is deep and pronounced. The voice box lies low and centered within the muscles and ligaments used to hold the head upright. The throat never feels rigid or tilted forward from under the jawline. Only then can a thin, unrestricted column of pressurized air push the tones freely up into the oral cavity and mask, to take full advantage of the resonating chambers.

Another Old Italian Master aphorism that can be directly attributed comes to us from the great Crescentini (1766–1846): "The art of singing is freedom about the neck, and the voice above the breath." In this regard, he does not mean that the head lolls from lack of support but rather that no muscles of the neck and throat feel tight.

Bel canto teacher Mancini approaches this situation from a negative point of view, but his quotation serves to remind us that they knew hundreds of years ago what prevented good singing:

> The voice cannot come out natural and spontaneous if it finds the throat in a strained position which impedes natural action. Therefore the student must take the trouble to accustom his chest to give the voice with naturalness and to use the throat smoothly and easily. If the union of these two parts reaches the point of perfection, then the voice will be clear and agreeable. But if these organs act discordantly, the voice will be defective and the singing will be spoiled. (Duey 1951, 104)

Speaking of the throat, Old Italian Master Maffei wrote that "Nothing should move while singing except the arytenoid cartilage" (Duey 1951, 38).

The chest doesn't need to heave, the face or jaw to work. Most important, only the automatic inner working of the throat should function, and this action is neither directly controllable nor felt. The throat is incredibly quiet, considering what it is accomplishing.

When we breathe correctly and the diaphragm is allowed to flatten like the head of a drum, the vocal apparatus inside the throat seems to collapse a bit. One of my teachers and an excellent singer, Elizabeth Mannion, said her throat feeling was like a bucket dropping down into a well, the well being the top of the trachea. The throat is not, however, consciously held down.

By standing in front of a mirror when breathing well, you will be able to note freedom of the neck and the larynx inside it. You will note no muscles or veins standing out on the sides, no pressing down or forward.

The bel canto teacher Maffei gives another reason to depend on a mirror: "People look ugly if they shake their heads while singing from the throat.... The singer should keep a mirror in front of him so as to know of any ugly gesture which he has made while singing" (Duey 1951, 38).

On a personal note, I will frankly say that my throat feelings are an absolute and unfailingly accurate barometer of how I am readying myself to sing. If I feel a totally open and low throat, I know that I have good control over my inspiration. If my throat feels at all caught or held, it is invariably an indication that I am tensing one or more sets of abdominal muscles and not allowing myself to relax into a deep inspiration and then fully set the chest and the rib muscles.

THE AUTOMATIC VOCAL CORDS

Clippinger, in *Fundamentals of Voice Training*, writes: "The action of the vocal cords is so largely automatic by reason of their close association with the life of the individual that any attempt to control them by direct effect would result in failure" (1929, 30).

My hero in this business is Shakespeare:

It is considered to be a task unnecessary to the student to enter more minutely into the action of the delicate muscles which separate and open widely the vocal cords when we breathe.... But what must be insisted on as of the highest importance is the necessity of leaving the throat, tongue, and jaw free to act in independence of each other. This condition can only be attained when the breath is properly controlled, and this independence constitutes the most effectual sign that the muscles inside the larynx are also free to perform their different functions. (1898, 23)

FIGURE 10

Anatomy of the voice box

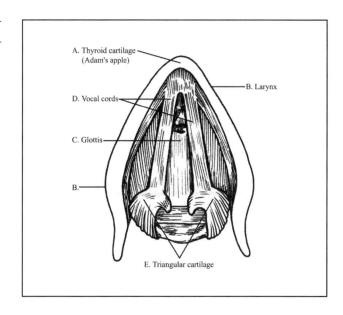

A. Thyroid cartilage (Adam's apple)

B. Larynx

D. Vocal cords

C. Glottis

B.

E. Triangular cartilage

Just so that you can hold your own in a so-called learned discussion with trained vocal coaches, Figure 10 shows, from above, the anatomy of the voice box. There are actually two sets of flaps that can vibrate in the respiratory channel. These are the *superior* (or *false*) *vocal cords* and the *inferior* (or *true*) *vocal cords*. (See the vertical larynx diagram, Figure 9.) The superior cords are not used for legitimate singing and are thought by some to come into play with the *feigned voice* or *falsetto voice*.

Some compare the inferior (i.e., lower) vocal cords to a reed instrument, some to strings, but Webster's International Dictionary states:

> Voice is produced by action of the vocal cords, not like the strings of a stringed instrument, but as a pair of membranous lips which being continually forced apart by the expired breath, and continually brought together again by their own elasticity and muscular tension, break the breath current into a series of puffs, or pulses, sufficiently rapid to cause the sensation of tone. The power, or loudness, of such a tone depends on the force of the separate pulses, and this is determined by the pressure of the expired air, together with the resistance of the vocal cords. The pitch depends upon the rapidity of these pulses.

ADDUCTION OF THE CORDS

A little bit of information here may help you understand the mechanism of the vocal cords and why you have an absolute bottom note and an absolute top note (I am sure you know that both are beyond the pleasant singing range of your voice). Each person's vocal cords are of a certain size and thickness. These factors determine your lowest tone. There is a point at which your cords will not vibrate any slower, no matter how much air blows by them. At the other extreme, the cords work in a special way to give you quite a few extra high notes. When they cannot be stretched any tighter or thinner, they begin to close in on themselves, from the back to the front. The opening for the air gets smaller and smaller. This is called *adduction*. (Refer to Figure 11 to see the conditions of the vocal cords at various pitches.) People cannot feel adduction happening, nor is it harmful in any way. Some theorists hypothesize that this modification of the cords results in a change of sound that can be heard, which they call the *head register*.

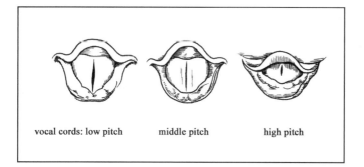

vocal cords: low pitch   middle pitch   high pitch

FIGURE 11

Conditions of the vocal cords at various pitches

VIBRATO, TREMOLO, WARBLE, BLEAT, AND WOBBLE

Vibrato is the natural occurrence in the voice of minute, cyclical variations in the intended pitch. It is caused by the variations of breath pressures emerging from the lungs, by automatic, millisecond adjustments of the vocal cords to hold a true tone, and probably by the very shapes of the laryngeal passages. In its optimal form, vibrato is a prized aspect of a voice and imparts some of the individuality that makes a singer popular. Violinists and other classical string players work to enrich the quality of their sounds by gently rocking their fingertips back and forth on the fingerboard during slow passages, copying this vocal quality.

Lack of control of the vibrato is most often caused by lack of proper breath control and the compensatory tightening of certain parts of the throat if this is not accomplished. Each type of breathing and throat tension contributes to a quality of vibrato, either good or bad.

A pleasing vibrato does not exceed one-quarter of a note from the target pitch. A vibrato moving back and forth beyond the space of a semitone or half pitch is perceived as annoying. At the same time, there is a matter of what is called *periodicity,* which is how often the cycle repeats itself. Too fast a vibrato is called a *tremolo, warble,* or *bleat,* and too slow is called a *wobble.* A "warbler" whose career was not hurt by her fast vibrato was Jeannette MacDonald, who sang in many movie musicals with Nelson Eddy soon after talkies began. Singers of advanced age, because of the general weakening of their muscles, sometimes develop a wobble. At the opposite extreme, there are singers who are able to sing with such a steady release of air that their tonal variation is less than a quarter pitch. This is called *straight tone,* and although one might think such control would be appreciated, most listeners do not like the sound any better than a pure tone sound propagated by an oscilloscope. Many choirmasters, however, like it for its purity and blending characteristics.

My bias toward the ideal number of cycles in a vibrato is 4.8 to 5.5 per second. According to Appelman, the ideal is "five to seven pulsations each second" (1974, 24). Knowing this, however, will avail you very little, because there is a natural optimal rate to your voice upon which you cannot effect adjustment. This is ordinarily not a matter to concern yourself about, other than to strive to keep the throat completely free.

It is interesting to note that the following singers had rather fast vibrato rates, and they were among the most celebrated operatic and concert performers of their times: Galli-Curci, 7.4; Caruso, 7.1; Martinelli, 6.8; Gigli, 6.3. They were, however, all from roughly the same bygone era, when tastes were different.

Cornelius L. Reid, in *Bel Canto: Principles and Practices,* expresses the belief that some control over vibrato is possible. He writes that

> Control over the vibrato...is maintained by the singer *indirectly* and is accomplished by regulating the intensity, or by simulating emotional effects.... Any voice movement in singing suitably described 'excessive,' whether it be too rapid and fluttery, or too slow and wobbly, stems from an entirely different arrangement and co-ordination of the voice parts and bear no relationship to the vibrato either as to cause or effect. Whereas the vibrato is always the result of a correctly functioning mechanism, the tremolo usually denotes the presence of throatiness, while the wobbly and unsteady tone show that the instrument is being unduly strained and overburdened by forcing for volume. (1950, 125–127)

As a word of advice, be careful of the vocal teacher who preaches control of vibrato or tremolo as part of the singer's course of study. The only kind of addressing of these should be of the nature of Wronski's advice: "Usually tremolo is the result of organic weakness, sickness, poor use of the breath, or stiffness of the vocal organs. If it is a fault of production, it can be corrected. Quick exercises are advisable for curing this defect" (1921, 64). In other words, learn to breathe in balance with the strong muscles of the body, learn to free the throat, and use pulsated drills and quick runs up and down the scale to apply your physical improvements.

CHAPTER 4

Resonance/The Head

IF ONE READS MANY SINGING GUIDES, one finds that *resonance* means different things to different people. To Salvatore Marchesi, "Resonance is caused when a sounding body communicates its vibrations to another body; or when, in other words, the second body is thrown into co-vibration with the first body" (1902, 27). This notion is at work when we say, "That idea resonates with me."

Marchesi might have liberalized his definition by saying, "also when a sounding body communicates vibrations to another part of the same body," as when the vibrations created in the larynx travel into the pharynx, oral, and nasal/sinus cavities. This is fundamentally what Clippinger states:

> The tone quality of the human voice, like that of other musical instruments, is dependent upon two things: a generator and a resonator. In the voice the vocal cords are the generator and the vocal cavities—pharynx, mouth, and head cavities, are the resonator, or resonators if one considers them separately.
>
> Resonance means that something is vibrating more or less sympathetically with the sound-waves sent out by the generator.
>
> The resonator does not originate sound. It takes what the generator sends it and makes the best it can of it. It cannot give out any tone that is not first received from the generator. The office of the resonator is to reinforce the tone and give it quality. (1929, 42)

I would argue that when we speak of human resonance, we are speaking about the filtering and reinforcement processes that occur to the complex spectrum of wavelengths that leave the larynx and travel up into and thence out of the head. This full spectrum of sounds, which I mentioned in Chapter 3, is also called *white noise*. (More about this later in this chapter.)

An interesting definition of *human resonance* is offered by D. Ralph Appelman as "the will to form a particular vowel position" (1974, 9). When you think about it, vowels are truly the carrying element of singing. Other than humming and a few so-called liquid consonants, if you want to prolong a sound from your throat, you do it on some vowel. (More about vowels later in the book.)

The more open the throat is, the greater the number of partials and long wavelengths can escape the *glottis* (the opening between the vocal cords). Now we are beginning to create by selecting from the full spectrum of light, the full palette of oils, the full box of crayons.

THE SCIENCE OF VOCAL SOUND

Without belaboring this issue, let me try to explain simply some of the acoustical science associated with singing. An analogy can be made that the vocal apparatus, primarily the vocal cords, is like a paint factory. This factory produces paints of many colors, shades, and tints. The colors we can think of as the different pitches, the tints as the partial tones contained within the pitches, and the shades as the relative loudness or softness of each tone.

When we command the voice to make a singing sound, our vocal cords produce a rich palette of tones of a certain intensity. If we place a mini-microphone down into the throat just above the cords, we are amazed to hear a cacophony of sounds akin to an untuned radio or to sleep machine noise. It is also akin to what is called *white noise*. This is a good image, because white light is actually all wavelengths of light and therefore all colors together. To get one particular color, other colors must be filtered out. It is not the job of the vocal cords to produce the end result our audience hears, but rather to offer a palette that the singer selects from, to create not just a tonal pitch but one with resonant beauty and intelligibility. This is the great advantage the singing voice has over every other instrument: by producing words, it conveys meaning as well as the intrinsic beauty of the music.

You have probably never thought before about how pure tone is made into intelligible *phonemes*—that is, the smallest elements of language that convey meaning. Generally, phonemes are like letters of the alphabet, but they may also be like a single syllable. The way this occurs is by the action of the tongue, jaw, lips, cheeks, and soft palate. These act in tandem to filter out unwanted sounds. (More on phonemes, vowels, and consonants later.)

Each tone emerging from the throat is made up of a *fundamental* (the basic pitch or note) and the so-called *partial tones* above it. The partials occur at the perfect fifth, and then the perfect fourth above that, and the major third, minor third, and even smaller partials beyond. The number of partials and their relative strengths determine the sound quality and the intelligibility of the sound. This, by the way, is why you can identify with your eyes closed a ram's horn, a French horn, and an English horn all producing exactly the same pitch. Each has its own particular blend of partials and intensities, somewhat like Marilyn Horne and Lena Horne each having a unique vocal signature.

There are two main segments or locations of the filtering process. The first is from immediately above the vocal cords and up along the pharynx to as far as the uvula dangling from the soft palate. The second is the mouth area, directly in front of this. These are called *first* and *second formants*. In varying proportions, they form the sustained sounds that we call vowels. We further use tongue, lips, and cheeks to create consonants. In Figure 12, we see a graphic representation of the combined cycles of vibration that mix to form what we perceive as vowels. In 1886, the International Phonetic Association developed the International Phonetic Alphabet, which provided symbols for every vowel, consonant, and common combination. We see in the graph a as in "tar," æ as in "sat," e as in "vacation," i as in "eat," and I as in "it." The graph numbers should be multiplied by 100 cycles per second. The inner circle around each vowel represents what is perceived as the purest production of the vowel, and the outer circle represents the extent to which each vowel will still be recognized as such. Thanks to the human ear, practice, and context, we therefore do not have to be perfect about producing vowels. Even more important, we clearly have latitude to color vowels in order to produce them higher in the resonating chambers. To be absolutely proper, the same male and female vowels have slightly different frequencies. This chart shows only approximate positions.

FIGURE 12

X–Y graph, locating vowels by means of combined formant pitches

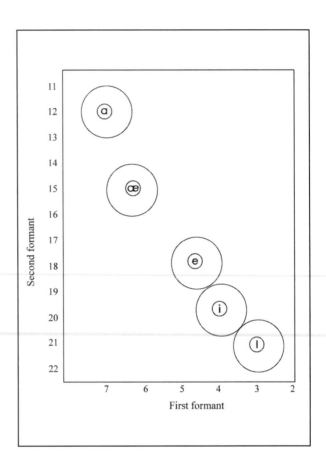

The laws of physics state that a pipe needs to be of a minimal width to allow certain wavelengths to operate inside it. If the pipe is too small, only small waves can pass through. The same law operates inside the "pipe" of our throat. Our job, therefore, is to allow the spaces to remain as wide open as possible without undue effort, to allow the passage of the richer, longer wavelengths.

When we use the strong muscles of the body rather than the tongue and jaw to control the airflow in singing, we have the luxury of keeping the throat/head system open. This openness is tantamount to driving your car on a four-lane city highway at four in the morning. When the tongue and jaw are clamped to help restrict expiration, this is like trying to get from Exit 2 to Exit 7 during peak rush hour. The frustration is equal.

ELEMENTS FOR MAXIMIZING RESONANCE

To create the largest, fullest, most sonorous tones, we must understand how the tongue, lips, jaw, mouth, and nasal cavities should act in singing and what might be preventing these actions.

THE TONGUE

It has been said that "The tongue is an unruly member." Nowhere is this more true than in singing. The first problem for most of us is that we have no idea how big the tongue is. Those who have seen a cow tongue hanging in a butcher shop (a common sight in Italy) know that it is akin to an iceberg: the part you see is the small part. We normally think of the tongue as that part called the *blade,* which is what waggles up and down, curls, dips, and flips inside our mouths. We see back to where it curves down under the uvula, and then we stop thinking about it. In fact, the big part of the tongue is under this curve. In Figure 13, you can see that the tongue fills a large area and is rooted directly above the opening to the windpipe.

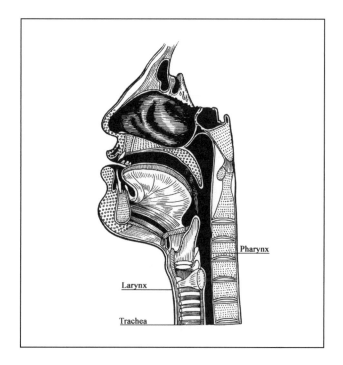

FIGURE 13

Side view of the tongue and resonating cavities

Pharynx

Larynx

Trachea

The Tongue as Resistance

"The guttural sound is noticed when the root of the tongue weighs on the epiglottis, and that organ is pushed into the path of the sonorous waves" (Garcia 1894, 17).

"The moment an attempt is made to sing with the end of the breath, the impossibility of rightly controlling it is felt by the singer, who becomes embarrassed by the throat assisting in this eking out process, and by the listener, who detects the absence of steadiness and the lack of fullness in the tone and intensity of the note" (Shakespeare 1898, 17). What Shakespeare is speaking of here is that when the breath is not controlled by the strong torso muscles or when a singer tries to sing on an exhausted breath, the bottom of the tongue creeps down into the throat to hold back what little air remains by making the epiglottis just below it into a gate. This is felt as tightness in the throat by the singer and perceived as weakness and tension in the sound by the listener.

Many amateur singers feel great tension under the angle of their lower jaw. They can't seem to get rid of it, as it happens to them automatically. This is especially true as they sing higher or louder.

We all understand that if singing is *extended speech on pitches,* then we must hold back our breath somehow to get to the end of the vocal line. If we do not understand how to do this with the strong muscles of the body, we are reduced to using a more brutal and injurious method called *retrograding* the tongue.

The base of the tongue, where it is rooted, sits just over the top opening of the throat, which is capped by the epiglottis. If we push the tongue down far enough, we will have a reflex coughing action to try to force it back up. We know that when we swallow, we need to cover the airway into the lungs so that food and liquids don't go down. We have all experienced when something "goes down the wrong way." This, of course, is because the same opening branches off to the esophagus and thence to the stomach and also to the larynx and thence to the trachea, bronchial tubes, and inner chamber of the lungs.

This same swallowing action that prevents things from getting down the larynx can also be used to prevent air from escaping up through the larynx. The tongue acts as the court of last resort in terms of holding back the air we need to sing long phrases. It works, to be sure, but it works poorly. This habit makes for what we call *throaty singing* at its worst. Done slightly, it still impedes the full range of overtones from escaping the throat and prevents the column of air from vibrating unimpeded toward the mouth and against the nasal and sinus cavities.

To add injury to insult, this pressing down of the back of the tongue creates a pressure that is bad for the delicate vocal cords and surrounding muscles. They are receiving unimpeded air power from beneath, which must be brutally countered by a back pressure caused by constriction immediately above. The muscles all around the top of the throat must tense to hold back the air. The cords are being overstressed. Eventually, this begins to hurt. Then, if not stopped, it makes the area numb. Then you become hoarse. Eventually, the vocal cords swell and become inflamed. At the worst, all singing is prevented and even speaking may be affected.

The tongue was not intended for this crude work in singing. In point of fact, the back of the tongue is not needed at all to control expiration. When the strong muscles of the torso are correctly used for the resistance to expiration pressure, the back of the tongue should rise out of the way and seem to float in stasis. This creates more room in the pharyngeal area and allows for the release of richer sound waves.

Terminology for Areas of Resonance

Some teachers wish to use common terms to help locate the areas of resonance in the head. Figure 14 is a drawing that names the areas. Be aware that *blade* is interchangeable with *tip* in describing the very front of the tongue.

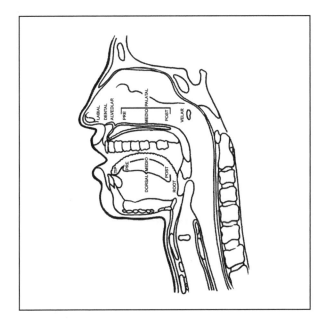

FIGURE 14

Parts of the head involved in singing

Position of the Tongue

"While sustaining a tone, the tongue must lie flat and quiet, and the front be pressed easily against the teeth" (Pfeiffer and Nageli 1890, 10).

"Whenever we sing any note, especially the highest notes of all the registers, the best sign that we have achieved perfection is that the tongue is left entirely free for pronunciation; and this is precisely what happens when we succeed in sustaining the voice with a rightly controlled breath" (Shakespeare 1898, 26).

In general during singing, the back of the tongue should rise as well out of the throat as is comfortable. Often, this means simply leaving it where it was at rest (with the lowered jaw creating the space). The blade of the tongue should be as free as possible. While at rest, the tip remains just where the bottom front teeth are rooted to the gums.

Bach writes,

> We expressly say 'with the tongue lying perfectly still and flat,' [because] ... if the epiglottis, by the retraction of the tongue, is firmly pressed down on the vocal cords ... it muffles the sound and makes the notes thick and dull. Beside, the tones lost resonance as the tongue is raised [in the front and retrograded in back]. On the other hand, with a flat position of the tongue [in the front], the epiglottis is lifted up, and the voice sounds clear and full, pure and brilliant. (1898, 35)

In Downing's view, "If the back of the tongue bunches up in the throat, it acts as an obstruction, making it impossible for the tone to pass freely into the mouth and head for resonance" (1927, 5–6).

For those students who push their tongue down, I counter the action by asking them to imagine that the front and back of the tongue form a shape like Cinderella's glass slipper—a shoe with a pronounced heel to it—the front being the toe. I liken the back of the tongue to an inflated helium balloon. A third image I use with students is the foil fencer's trailing forearm when not thrusting, dangling beside his head with elbow high and hand low and loose.

Now, if you try to speak with the tongue in this position, you sound as if you have a speech impediment. However, when you sing and extend your vowels, this quality vanishes.

Lilli Lehmann devotes an entire section of her book to the tongue:

> It has an extremely delicate and difficult task to perform. It must be in such a position as not to press either upon the larynx or epiglottis.

Tongue and larynx must keep out of each other's way, although they always work in coöperation; but one must not hamper the other, and when one can withdraw no farther out of the way, the other must take it upon itself to do so. For this reason the back of the tongue must be raised high, the larynx stand low. (1924, 150)

THE JAW

The jaw can be and often is used incorrectly in conjunction with the tongue to help hold back airflow. This is done by drawing it down with the mandibular (jaw) and upper throat muscles and then locking it in place or even by sliding it down and forward. The higher and/or louder the imperfect singer sings this way, the more she or he will note in a mirror that the jaw moves.

The opposite needs to be true in good singing. **The jaw should at all times be relaxed. It is best if this relaxation is done directly from the jaw's hinges just in front of the ears.** We call this *unhinging,* although the bone stays in the sockets. The muscles simply relax, and the jaw lowers. Holding the jaw backward with effort, however, is not a good remedy.

Shakespeare goes so far as to say that "It would be possible to learn to sing merely by producing the voice with the jaw absolutely loose and to a right breath-control" (1898, 29).

According to Downing,

A rigid jaw is perhaps the singer's greatest enemy. There is nothing which will handicap clear enunciation or produce a more metallic tone quality, than a rigid jaw.

To relax the jaw, think of loosening the muscles at the angle of the jaw below the ears, these being the muscles that tighten the jaw. Relax these muscles and let the jaw hang ... Keep the upper and lower back jaw well separated. This position allows more space in the mouth and throat and enriches the tone quality. (1927, 8)

Stella Owsley writes,

Drop the lower jaw from its base under the ears, as though it swings on a hinge. The tongue [blade] always follows the loose jaw and rests slightly curved under behind the front lower teeth. . . . A loose lower jaw will cause the mouth to be opened about a thumb's breadth. A too wide mouth will press down the chin onto the larynx and contract the breath passage. In dramatic passages the mouth is opened a bit wider. Lamperti, a famous early Italian singer, used to say, 'He who moves the mouth will never become a singer.' (1937, 65)

Lilli Lehmann, in speaking about making head tones, describes "the gentle downward relaxation of the chin. It is drawn very far backward so that the tongue stands high out of the throat and that the larynx may move freely under the tongue" (1924, 54).

Few teachers speak of such blatant manipulation of the jaw/chin as recommended by Lehmann, but the point here is that **the jaw cannot be allowed to move forward and set firmly. Nor can the tongue move in concert with it downward in the back. This is simply a bad compensatory habit for controlling high breath pressure when the strong muscles of the torso fail to do the work.**

I give my students the mental image of the jaw lowering like a plumber's wrench or spanner. This tool is adjusted by a wheel that is turned. The two jaws move apart parallel to each other. I ask students to imagine the jaw hanging straight down or even slightly back. I use the image of pliers opening to provide an illustration of the incorrect lowering of the jaw.

Duey records that

> Part and parcel with stance, the jaw should work freely on a head looking easily out to the horizon. The French bel canto teacher Jumilhac (1611–1682) observed that the head and chin should not be lowered too much, in order that it not interfere with the articulation of the syllables and the clear pronunciation of the words. (1951, 68)

Without good stance, good breathing is difficult. Without good breathing, proper resistance is very difficult. Without a high tongue and unhinged jaw, resonating fully in your nasal cavity is impossible.

THE LIPS

The lips should also be relaxed, to accomplish their job without undue effort. The lips are rarely a problem in singing. In general, a Mona Lisa smile helps tone and is also pleasing to the audience. This smile, parenthetically, I find to be conveyed as much by slightly elevated cheeks and "smiling eyes" as by the lips.

One of my graduate school teachers, Elizabeth Mannion, offered an interesting insight. She said, "Did you ever wonder why Marilyn Monroe's lips when she got ready to kiss were so much sexier than anyone else's? The reason is that she didn't pucker locally from the lips but rather relaxed her lips languidly forward from her ears and through her cheeks. This is the same way we should adjust our lips for singing." I have always found this to work for myself and my students.

The Old Italian Masters used to say, "A tone is a flower of the lips." They meant that this is the place where tone seems to blossom or focus, but they also suggested that the lips should look as pleasing to the audience as do flowers.

THE MOUTH OPENING

"The old Italian school says that the singer should open the mouth as far as to be able to place his forefingers between the teeth" (Bach 1898, 28).

The most common statement set down by masters teaching singing between 1777 and 1927 is that the mouth should not be opened too wide. Many during this period also recommended the "gently smiling mouth," but this advice has fallen out of favor in the twentieth and twenty-first centuries.

In Garcia's guide, he asks the question, "Should the mouth be opened wide as a means of obtaining power and beauty of sound?" and answers his own question, "This is a common error. The mouth should be opened by the natural fall of the jaw. This movement, which separates the jaws by the thickness of a finger and leaves the lips alone, gives the mouth an easy and natural form. . . . The real mouth of a singer ought to be considered the Pharynx" (1894, 12).

Garcia's statement is acoustically very sound. **The laws of acoustics dictate that the mouth's cross-sectional opening cannot benefit from being any wider than the cross-sectional area of the back of the mouth to sing.** Therefore, to open it like a vampire about to feed has no purpose and will probably yield a poorer sound because of pressing down over the larynx. In singing loudly, however, the mouth does open incrementally wider.

THE TEETH

The teeth are of no concern at all in singing—unless you don't have them. My first voice teacher had dentures, and they (as well as his advanced age) severely hampered his ability to sing. Caruso was convinced that if he lost his teeth he would lose his career. Clearly, the teeth shape the oral cavity and naturally hold the mouth in the correct position. They are also important to the singer in conveying a pleasant demeanor when performing. Singing is, therefore, yet one more compelling reason to take good care of one's teeth.

Hiller (1728–1804) was one of the earliest writers on singing to observe and advance the "gentle smile." He suggests that the singer's face should bear the expression of a gentle smile with the mouth drawn slightly to the sides and the lips not reared back tensely to show the upper teeth but revealing only a bit of the lower teeth. The mouth is generally open about the width of the pinkie finger turned sideways (Duey 1951, 67). The great Luciano Pavarotti is one among a number of professional singers who expose their lower teeth when singing loudly or in the upper part of the voice. This can be a reflex action of lifting the soft palate and slightly lowering the jaw while consciously not wanting to push the jaw or tongue down.

THE PALATES

The hard palate is the formation of bone and mucus membrane that separates the front of the nasal cavity from the mouth (refer to Figure 13). Attached directly behind it and seamlessly connected is the soft palate, so named because it feels softer and is not bone and so is slightly moveable. Together, these are also called the *roof of the mouth*. It is the very important equivalent to an acoustic keyboard instrument's soundboard. And yet nothing can be done locally to affect the hard palate for singing. The soft palate can be raised slightly. If the soft palate is overrelaxed, a quality some country-and-western singers such as Willie Nelson cultivate, an extra amount of airflow and tone gets into the back of the nasal cavity and creates what we call *nasal singing* or *twang.*

The soft palate can be lifted somewhat when the singer wants to cultivate a "rounder" tone on low notes and a brighter, more ringing tone on upper notes. This is the feeling we get when we prepare to sneeze. Lilli Lehmann recommended raising the soft palate for the so-called head tones, which are the high end of a singer's range (1924, 20). This seems reasonable, as these tones are under such pressure that their vibratory abilities can be better imparted to the resonating cavities than low ones. Tightening the soft palate makes it pass the vibrations better upward, helping to create a brilliant ring to the tones.

Novello (1856) and Bassini (1857) are early proponents of raising the soft palate, saying that this, in tandem with keeping the larynx low, increases the size of the resonating cavity. Thorp and Nicholl concur in 1899. In my doctoral study, thirty-two teachers suggested raising the soft palate, and nine opposed the concept. I personally find that trying to do this for any length of time is exhausting. I, therefore, preach its discrete use for tone coloring and to make high notes ring.

THE NASAL/SINUS CAVITIES

There is no direct control of the nasal cavities except to allow more sound to pass through the pharynx. This does not mean, however, that this part of the voice is unimportant; it is very important. It is to the human instrument what the case is to a grand piano. Without this, the piano is basically a harp on its side. Compare the power of the sounds of the harp and the piano. Or you may think of the hollow construction of all the string instruments of the orchestra. These vibratory chambers are what reinforce the dulcet, mellow sounds, or actually select the dulcet elements from the vibrations created by a bow drawn across or fingers plucking strings.

You understand how important the nasal cavities are when you have a bad head cold. Everyone knows, even over the telephone, in speaking with you that your head is stuffed up, because you lose a great portion of your resonance.

The Need for Open Space

Although these collective cavities, called together the *nasal and sinus cavities,* cannot be altered by muscular effort, their potential to reinforce beautiful sound can be created by us allowing more of the waves generated by our vocal cords to get to them. Again, this requires that the "pipeline" be as open as possible. Remember that it makes no difference if you have a four-lane highway from points H to Z in the journey of your tones if points A to G are along a one-lane dirt road. The entire path from vocal cords to your nose and lips must be open.

Without a firm breath resistance, a thin stream of highly pressurized air cannot be generated to pass unimpeded through the larynx and pharynx and thence bounce tones against the palates, creating sympathetic vibrations in the head cavities. Low or restricted breath pressure confines the tones to the back of the throat and mouth and their soft, absorbent tissues. High pressure vibrates the high open chambers and imparts the brilliant ring of the professional singer.

THE EYES

Like Irish eyes, the singer's eyes should be smiling, unless the mood of the words and/or music dictates otherwise. The eyes, as da Vinci said, are the windows of the soul. They will certainly telegraph tension in the face if it is there. Check in the mirror. If the muscles around the eyes are tense, support with the torso muscles and relax the muscles in the head.

OTHER CONSIDERATIONS CONCERNING RESONANCE

PROPRIOCEPTIVE HEARING

The term *proprioceptive hearing* means "to hear from yourself." In singing, it means that you hear not only through your ears, but also through the inside of your head. In fact, because your ears are on the sides of your head and intended to pick up outside sounds, they are not especially well placed to hear your voice. This placement, coupled with the hearing of your voice picked up from the inside, gives you a sensation of your own sound different than others receive. You know this if you have ever heard a recording of yourself. Invariably, the sound is less rich than you are used to. Between bone conduction and whatever might come up the inner ear canals, you are getting much more of the lower frequencies emanating from your pharynx.

The real problem comes when singers depend on proprioceptive hearing to judge not just the quality of their sound, but also its size. Merely by tightening the mucus membranes inside the pharynx, like stretching a drumhead tighter, more low tones will be passed directly to the inner ear. But this tightening makes the "pipe" smaller. Ironically, although you think you are making a richer and louder sound, you are producing a tighter sound in which less escapes to the outside and thus to your audience.

Frequently when my pupils have begun to sing more freely, they complain that their sound has grown smaller. I prove to them this is not true by putting them in front of a tape recorder, then playing back. They can judge their vocal strength relative to the piano. This is one of the most important reasons to put oneself in the hands of a vocal coach you can trust. During the critical period between tense and free singing, the singer is not in a position to correctly judge the quality and intensity of his or her sound production.

FOCUSING SOUND

A major objective in beautiful singing is to place the tones *forward* and *high*. By this, we mean that they sound like they are filling the front of the mouth and vibrating in the nasal cavity just above. This is the objective behind the Old Italian Master adage "A tone is a flower of the lips." The target area is called the *mask,* and it is located precisely where you would wear a costume ball mask, or the one worn by the Lone Ranger or Zorro. This area resonates precisely as the box for a violin does.

The celebrated teacher Margaret Harshaw used to take her two index fingers and create a horizontal *V* pointing away from her, just in front of her nose, to demonstrate where the point of *focus* should be. Many teachers agree that the phenomenon of excellent resonation seems to place the focal point of tones just in front of the nose or the philtrum, that little groove that runs from your nose to your upper lip. And yet, there are no mechanisms inside the head other than the tongue, lips, jaw, and soft palate for helping to attain focus. These work in concert to produce the higher, "purer" vowels, such as the Italian "ah, eh, ih, oh, oo." In my opinion, it is better to use this phenomenon as a measuring instrument than a working tool.

The pronounced tonal difference perceived by audiences between mediocre and good singers is largely attributable to the amount of tone vibrated in the resonating chambers of the head. The more dynamic resistance that can be brought to bear from the upper torso and the middle sides and lower-middle back balancing the pressure from the abdominal area, the more energized the air column can be that creates the tones. The more energized the air, the higher the tones rise through the open throat and pharynx into the head, and the more they are reinforced by the hollow cavities.

THE HEAD AND THE HORIZON

As a rule, it is best to hold the head so that the eyes are looking straight forward to the horizon. This position may, of course, be modified, for dramatic purpose, but either looking too far up or lowering the head too far down puts strain or pressure unnecessarily on the throat. Some singers tilt the head slightly down, and this is better in my estimation than is slightly up.

Some students turn their heads in an attempt to hear themselves better. This, of course, never works, as the ears go with the rest of the head. Some cup their hands to their ears. This is a habit to be avoided. When the time comes to perform without your cupping hand, you feel as if it had been amputated, and you will not be sure of your tone quality.

THE YAWN

As you begin to relax the tongue, jaw, cheeks, and lips, you may find yourself yawning. I have had many pupils do this after the first few weeks of study. Several teachers, including the great Garcia, have advised either yawning or imagining yawning to create an open throat. Here are two representative quotations:

"The sensation of freedom in the throat should be 'as before drinking' or 'as before yawning'" (Shakespeare 1910, 14).

"Most of my readers have yawned once or twice in their lives; if they will do it once more, in front of the looking-glass, and watch the inside of the mouth as they yawn, they will see and feel the exact position in which the throat should be during good singing" (Crowest 1900, 56).

If you find yourself yawning constantly, however, get more rest!

PROOF THAT THESE PRACTICES WORK: THE SNEEZE

All of the above may sound reasonable to you, but is there a higher authority than myself that you can avail to check out these theories? There is. It is your own body, obeying the laws of nature and self-preservation.

Consider the sneeze. We know that the sneeze is the body's reflex response to defend itself from airborne objects it considers harmful, such as dust, pollen, or bacteria. To ensure they leave the respiratory system, the act of expulsion is quite violent. It is so violent that if it's not done correctly, harm can be done to the delicate vocal apparatus. So nature adjusts and prepares.

Every one of us has had some wag bless us even before we sneeze because our facial expression telegraphs what is about to happen. Our jaw relaxes and hangs down limply (not thrust forward), so that our mouth opens. The front of our tongue stays low, but the back rises out of our throat, so that there will be no chance of resistance to the violent expulsion to come. The cheeks relax, and the soft palate rises. Only then do we let go. Sometimes it's incredibly loud and violent. But no harm comes to our vocal cords, because everything was gotten out of the way of the path from lungs to lips.

Therefore, in a modified way, we should think of the position of a sneeze whenever we prepare to sing. This position, however, will work only if you use the strong muscles of the torso to balance pressure and resistance.

DIAGNOSTICS

PROBLEM: When I begin to relax my throat and my head for singing, I find myself yawning.

ANSWER: That's no problem. It's a natural reaction to relaxation. Unless you're also tired, it will stop after a few minutes.

PROBLEM: I really try to relax my jaw and tongue, but I can get them to relax only so much.

ANSWER: Seek the rest of the relaxation elsewhere. The more you can let go of the tightness of the abdominal muscles, the more everything above your clavicles will relax. This is called *reflex action.*

I use with students an illustration of how focusing on another part of the body may produce interesting changes. When I visited Hawaii, I attended an islander show featuring hula dancers. The women were able to shake their hips incredibly quickly and make their grass skirts fly up and down. They invited men and women guests onstage to try the same and, of course, the guests couldn't emulate the speed. Then the hula ladies revealed the secret: don't try to shake your hips quickly; relax your knees and shake them quickly, and the hips come along for the ride. If you wish to relax the throat, tongue, and jaw, let go of the abdominal muscles before you begin to let in a breath.

I have had students work this backward, as well. They kept concentrating on "having no throat"—relaxing in that region so much that they couldn't feel any tension at all. The reflex action for them was to feel the muscles below the breastbone gradually relax.

PROBLEM: I think I've conquered good breathing, and I have a relaxed tongue and jaw when I begin to sing. As I ascend to the top end of my range, however, my tongue drops, my jaw comes forward, and I tighten up anyway.
ANSWER: If you are not unbalancing your pressure and resistance in the torso, the reason is probably old habit. Some people give up their "set" torso position as they ascend the scale. They need to refuse to do this. The Old Italian Masters said, "When you sing up, think down." However, you can still maintain your resistance on high notes but find your tongue and jaw lowering and tightening. As I have stated before, although you can't sing well with poor physical technique, this does not necessarily guarantee you will sing well with good breath control. Your mind remembers how your tongue and jaw were at those pitches before you improved your breath technique, and even if you don't know how high you're singing, the subconscious mind does. Actually, with my students I find that they will often sing freely until they are told or themselves realize how high they are singing. Then, in a panic, they revert to old ways. They "psych themselves out," as they tell me. In this case, it is best to work up the scale slowly and not try to sing high tones until you have mastered medium-high tones.

PROBLEM: During practice, I began to keep my hand on my throat so I could feel if I was tensing, and now I'm having trouble keeping my hand at my side.
ANSWER: Use a mirror instead, until you can feel the correct condition internally (which is "no throat"). Stop using the mental crutch of your hand immediately.

OBSERVATIONS ON HABITS AND SELF-CRITICISM

Here are three notes that apply for all of singing but that apply particularly to observation of the tongue, lips, and jaw. The first is that it is very difficult just to abandon an old habit. Generally, the best method of discarding any habit is to replace it proactively with a new habit. This is why people who try to quit cigarette smoking instinctively feel that they need something like gum to chew on. When you zero in on a problem, consult the appropriate part of this book for correct technique, get a picture of what you should be doing fixed in your mind, and make this your new habit.

The second admonition works in tandem with the first. Forget the bad habit, and concentrate on the good habit that will replace it. Above all, do not consciously (even if only inside your head) say to yourself: "Don't pull up" or "Don't tighten your jaw." This only results in what is called *negative reinforcement*. Focus on what you should do, not what you should not.

Finally, refrain from coaching yourself out loud. This can also become an unpleasant habit that is hard to break.

CHAPTER 5

Range and Timbre

RANGE IN SINGING

PEOPLE WHO ARE UNTRAINED AND KNOW ENOUGH about the scale will sometimes claim that they have only a one-octave range. On the opposite end, Julie Andrews boasted of having three singable octaves, and a mysterious woman who went by the name of Yma Sumac (some said she was spelling Amy Camus backward) claimed to have a four- (some say five-) octave range.

Everyone has two ranges in singing. The first is what I call *artistic range*. It is a predominant part of what determines an alto or mezzo, bass or tenor. This range encompasses the notes that an audience would be pleased to hear. It can often be widened by a diligent and correct study of voice.

The second is *natural range*. This range is terminated by the lowest pitch at which air passing the vocal cords can make them vibrate and the highest pitch before the vocal cords close in on themselves. With both of these, some people use the term *vocal compass*. Figure 15 shows vocal compasses by category.

Again, by observing physics, anatomy, and acoustics, we realize that every instrument has its limitations, the human voice included. Every set of cords has a certain thickness. There is a point below which the cords will not vibrate but will simply lie dormant as low-pressure air passes across them (clearly, normal inhaling and exhaling do not make the cords vibrate). This is the bottom of your natural range.

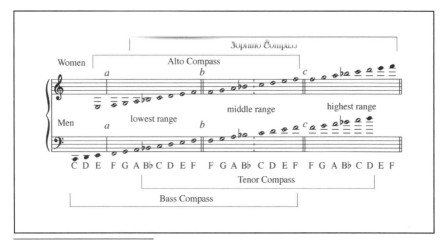

FIGURE 15

Vocal compasses by category

For the middle tones in a person's range, the cords create pitches by stretching. When the cords cannot stretch any more, they begin to close in on themselves in a process called *adduction*. Finally, there is only a tiny hole left. This is one's highest pitch. Then the cords close up. Pleasant sounds, however, vanish below this point.

For the normal person, a two-octave range limit is usual and more than adequate. The *ambitus* or range from low to high of the average song is usually not more than an octave and a half.

When studying singing, the desire to increase range should always take a back seat to producing a narrow scale properly. Unless one can sing the most comfortable octave with ease and resonance, working on widening the range downward and especially upward can result in strain or ruin to the voice.

ASPECTS OF RANGE

REGISTERS

Since people first began to teach singing, right up to this very day, a polite war has been raging in the vocal musical community about a thing called *registers*. Each register is supposedly a series of sounds in the singer's range with similar quality. Most who divide the voice into these groups believe that there are only two human registers: chest and head.

Manuel Garcia believed that "Every voice is formed of three distinct portions, or registers, namely *chest, medium,* and *head.* The chest holds the lowest place, the medium the middle, the head the highest. These names are incorrect, but accepted" (1894, 7).

Garcia flourished at the height of the fury about registers. Here is how he defines them:

> A register is a series of consecutive homogeneous sounds produced by one mechanism, differing essentially from another series of sounds equally homogeneous produced by another mechanism, whatever modifications of *timbre* and of strength they may offer. Each of the three registers has its own extent and sonority, which varies according to the sex of the individual, and the nature of the organ. (1894, 8)

So much focus was placed on registers that even the perceived point of passage was given a name: *il ponticello,* which in Italian means "the little bridge." In English, these tones were sometimes called *lifts.*

What causes these perceptible groupings of timbre in a voice? Ralph Appelman writes, "The exact cause of registration in the singing voice is unknown" (1967, 86). I will grant that the low end of any singer's voice has tones that sound "heavier and darker" as opposed to "lighter and more brilliant" on the top end. I venture a guess that the cause is complex, a combination of the predisposition of muscle, bone, and cavities to resonate; the varying shape and tilt of the vocal cords and laryngeal "box"; the phenomenon of adduction; and undoubtedly the increased pressure to produce higher tones that naturally drives the "head" tones more effectively into the resonating chambers of the sinuses. Perceptible timbre differences are the natural, subconscious adjustment of a wonder instrument that has the flexibility to change to produce a wide range of tones. What we hear are these modifications. Just because we can perceive them does not mean that we need to do anything about it. Many chapters, however, have been written about how to blend registers. Again, proper singing is the simple answer. Singers have sung beautifully for centuries ignorant of this debate.

Appelman correctly writes, "Professional singers more than teachers tend to believe that vocal registers do not exist" (1967, 86). I believe the reason for this discrepancy is that when breathing, phonation, and resonating are well done, Mother Nature takes over and thankfully handles this phenomenon automatically. **Whether or not there are two or three registers, if the voice is in perfect balance, no conscious control is necessary.**

Sir Morell Mackenzie, a pioneer in the understanding of the vocal apparatus, to my mind put it best in his book *The Hygiene of the Vocal Organs:* "A register is a series of tones of like quality producible by a particular adjustment of the vocal cords." Note that he did not say a particular conscious adjustment by the singer of the vocal cords.

Clippinger has a different belief, but he also comes to the conclusion that good singing is sufficient to handle the phenomenon:

If there had always been the right sense of freedom in the vocal instrument it is altogether likely that 'registers' would never have been heard of. Such things are the result of accumulation of tension.

With one adjustment of the vocal cords the singer can, by adding tension, produce a series of four or five tones. By that time he has reached the limit of tension with that adjustment and he makes a sudden change to another adjustment and produces another series of four or five tones. These sudden readjustments are what are called changes of register. (1929, 31)

Clippinger also writes,

The number of registers in the human voice as given by the writers of books varies from none at all to half a dozen or so. In the perfectly produced voice one would not go far wrong to say that there are no registers or that there are as many as there are tones in the compass, for in such a voice each tone has its own particular adjustment. (1929, 33)

Amazingly, Clippinger nonetheless goes on for pages about various registers!

Lilli Lehmann, who had a storied singing career, writes, "There are no vocal registers.... Do registers exist by nature? No" (1924, 107). She adds, "As long as the word 'register' is kept in use, the registers will not disappear. And yet, the register question must be swept away, to give place to another class of ideas, sounder views on the part of teachers, and a truer conception on the part of singers and pupils" (112). I agree with Lehmann regarding how to react to this question. She also states elsewhere that certain parts of the range of a singer sound differently, based on natural use of the larynx, tongue, and palate and in the extent of resonance in the cavities. I concur.

FALSETTO

The way many people sing into the high end of their range is by employing a control that is called *falsetto*. This has also been called the *feigned voice*. It is sometimes cultivated with considerable breath power behind it by men who wish to sing the castrati repertoire of the baroque era. They call themselves *countertenors*. The most prevalent theory of the mechanism of this high, pure sound is that the muscles around the larynx draw down and bring the ventricle bands, sometimes called the *superior* or *false vocal bands,* close to the true vocal bands, so that they, too, vibrate. The sound of the true bands is augmented; therefore, they do not need to vibrate with as much amplitude.

I have never investigated this phenomenon, because most of these upper tones can be produced "full voice," simply by applying the same rules of open throat and balance of pressure and resistance used throughout the vocal range. The downside of this technique is that the cultivation of falsetto virtually guarantees a voice will have two distinctly different, unblended "registers."

THE BREAK

Many singers experience at one time or another the cracking of a note when they tighten too much, when they are singing high, or when their breath balance fails. This is sometimes called *breaking.*

There is another vocal use for the term *break.* This one is the perceived no-man's-land of difficult notes between the chest and head registers. It is a curious phenomenon that cannot be swept under the table. However, again, **balanced control of the singing voice will carry the singer back and forth over the break with no other manipulation necessary.** For all singers, this break lurks around the middle C on the piano. This means that it occurs toward the bottom of the female's vocal range and the top of the male's. Logically, it is more vexing for tenors and contraltos, because they spend a great deal of their vocal time in this part of the scale. Several elements of the voice must be adjusted to sing different parts of the range, and at the break is where it is most felt and most often ill-handled. Once the body is in balance, however, these adjustments must be automatic.

A third use of the word break is to describe mutation of the voice from boy to man. This has nothing to do with the middle definition, but it does sound like the first one and was immortalized in the song "The Telephone Hour" from *Bye Bye Birdie.*

TIMBRE AND ITS TWO MEANINGS

Webster's New World Dictionary (Second College Edition) defines *timbre* as "the characteristic quality or sound that distinguishes one voice or musical instrument from another or one vowel sound from another; it is determined by the harmonics of the sound and is distinguished from the *intensity* and *pitch.*" (By the way, it's pronounced TAM-burr.)

From this definition, we see that we have two issues to speak about. The first is the quality of voice you received from nature. Not only might you be a bass-baritone, but if you are of African ancestry rather than European or Asian, you may have wider cheekbones and nasal area. If so, this facial structure will help impart more of that dulcet timbre that makes James Earle Jones's voice so distinguishable. Obviously, unless you undergo some major surgery, this timbre will not change.

Stanley writes,

> One does not train a voice as a soprano, or contralto, or any thing else. One merely starts poising the voice and getting it on timbre and the body [that is, the pressure and resistance controlled by the strong muscles of the body—BJM] under it, and then—the voice reveals itself and goes up or down and becomes deeper and richer or more brilliant, according to its individual character. (1916, 20–21)

There is a second meaning of *timbre,* which has to do with an individual singer changing the color of his or her sounds. **The timbre of vowels can be changed from dark to bright, or, as singing teachers say, from** *closed* **to** *open.* According to Garcia, the general production of bright or open tones is created by lowering the soft palate and allowing the larynx to rise. The dark, somber, or closed version of a tone involves raising the soft palate and lowering the larynx. This creates a larger rear area of resonance, the so-called first formant region. Another cause of darkening comes about because the pharyngeal area is relaxed, thus damping the bright overtones.

Most people instinctively manage a passable job of coloring their vowels. For those who do not, rather than trying to reason out complex mental adjustments for the dark and bright version of each vowel, I believe the singer and teacher together can listen to production and create desired qualities on a subconscious level.

WIDENING THE RANGE

As stated earlier, each singer has an optimal range and a wider natural range limited by his or her physiognomy. In the early years of training, the central octave should be the site of virtually all work. As time goes on, tones can be added upward and downward. For the young singer, age will strengthen the vocal muscles, cartilages, and ligaments so that more pressure may be applied without injury. Generally, before about age twenty-one in a male and eighteen in a female, the highest tones should not be used often; nor should the most taxing repertoire be introduced.

A technique that allows you to sing lower with loudness is to give the bottom few notes more airflow. This will not be done to a wasteful or breathy point, but the relatively thicker cords need more air mass to pass them in order to be activated. Poor singers can get large low notes by bearing down with the jaw and tongue, but this does not produce the best tones and instills a bad habit that soon may be carried upward.

Here is Taylor's similar take on this: "There is always a temptation to try to make low notes heavy and round. Yielding to this temptation results only in making the tones throaty and robbing them of their normal carrying power. Less muscular effort is required, the lower you sing" (1914, 55).

On the high end, the trick is less air but air under high pressure, with a perfect balance of breath pressure and resistance. The highest notes are produced by a thin filament of pressurized air. Large puffs under high pressure would need to be restrained, and the temptation or, worse, reflex action will be to lower the epiglottis with the jaw and tongue muscles to hold the air back.

Myer says,

> The untrained voice is usually in an unnatural condition, and the quality and compass cannot always be depended upon to decide surely and correctly the style or natural order of the voice. Commence study as nearly as possible about the middle of the compass of the voice, or on the best tones of the voice.... As the voice gains strength and action ... it will finally seek and finds its proper level and quality. (1891, 327–328)

Caruso also suggested starting with the middle range (1909, 51).

BEYOND RANGE AND TIMBRE

Range and timbre alone are not enough to classify voices. There is a matter of power, as well. Some people simply have more strength than others, bigger mouths and chests, and bigger nasal and sinus cavities, and they put these features to use in singing.

"Before everything, it is essential that the true quality of the voice should be once and for all determined. This is the keystone of the arch.... It is not always, however, an easy matter to recognize the natural order in which a given voice belongs.... Mere pitch is not a safe guide" (Mackenzie 1886, 160–161).

Owing to range, timbre, and strength/intensity, each classical singer is divided into category or, as the Germans say, *Fach*. For example, there is the soubrette soprano, as well as the lyric, the spinto, the dramatic, and the Wagnerian, in order from lightest to heaviest tone characteristics. Among sopranos there also is a special class called *coloratura,* for those who can sing extremely high. Such voices are almost invariably lighter rather than dramatic. Not infrequently as singers age, they move from a lighter to a heavier class. Voices do darken as people grow older. This darkening can occur because the cords get thicker from usage or because people naturally put on weight, and even the laryngeal and pharyngeal areas change size. The change in size, strength, and color, sometimes collectively called *weight,* of voice over time is such a natural phenomenon that composers use it in operas and musicals. Naturally, for tonal variety and for the sake of ensemble work, they wish to have a mix of vocal timbres and ranges in their work. To jibe with life, they make the old men basses, the middle-age men baritones, and the young men tenors. The same is done with female vocal types according to age.

Occasionally, singers will shift their careers into an entirely different major timbre, such as lyric to dramatic soprano. Some even change their category, usually pushing up a few notes into the next highest group. Many ruin their voices in the attempt. Others have such perfect control that they can accomplish it. Tenor Enrico Caruso once substituted for the indisposed baritone Scotti, and the audience was supposedly none the wiser. This is because Caruso naturally possessed the weight and some of the lower notes of a baritone in his voice. Similarly, the wonderful Placido Domingo is a more robust tenor than the equally wonderful Luciano Pavarotti. Domingo could have chosen a baritone career, except that he had the skill and strength to sing the higher repertoire, which provided more fame and money and perhaps more fun, too.

TRANSPOSING

An alternative to singing songs out of your range is to transpose them. This means to perform them in a lower or higher key. Most popular sheet music is written in the treble clef, for either mezzo-sopranos or baritones, because these are the most common voice ranges (mezzo means "middle"). As a tenor,

I usually transpose standard sheet music up, as much as a major third. I have been greatly aided by two developments of the modern age: the electronic keyboard and the music software program. Many electronic keyboards have the ability to transpose into virtually any other key. I also have a music writing computer program that can transpose an entire piece automatically to any other key on command. You will find as a performer that the change of key by as little as one-half tone can be significant in terms of wear and tear on your voice, as every note you sing will be affected. You will sound better singing a song with a brilliant climax if you place it at the high end of your usable range. If you are singing something like Cole Porter's "In the Still of the Night," placing the initial low notes perfectly in the strong low end of your voice will enhance the performance. You will also find, however, if you have a sensitive ear, that certain songs don't sound intrinsically good in certain keys. This observation dates back all the way to the time of the ancient Greek philosophers (although they were speaking as much about modes as keys). Also, your accompanist may refuse to play something written in a key with five flats or sharps. Trial, error, and common sense are the watchwords here.

CHAPTER 6

Singing and Health

OVERVIEW

IN GENERAL, THE RECOMMENDATIONS OF YOUR PHYSICIAN, of the surgeon general, and of reams of magazine articles about health apply for singing, as well. To enjoy life to the maximum, you should exercise regularly, eat plenty of fruits and vegetables, drink lots of water, avoid excess sugars and carbohydrates, and get enough sleep. Lack of sleep can have a perceptible effect on vocal cords. Remember that diaphragmatic and intercostal breathing—which occurs during sleep—relaxes the nervous system, enriches the blood with oxygen, and is even thought to massage the heart.

As I have noted elsewhere in this guide, there are many overweight people who sing well. My pet theory is that the excess pounds around their middle tend to cause them to relax their abdomens on inspiration and prevent them from drawing up, as in clavicular breathing. Research has also shown that excess fat sheathing nerve fibers makes people less jumpy and may contribute to the "jolly fat person" cliché, but neither of these speculations justifies becoming or staying overweight.

If the Old Italian Masters 350 years ago knew how to sing well, the ancient Greeks knew what constituted a good life thousands of years ago. I already stated that over one pediment of their most sacred temple in Delphi, they inscribed the maxim "Do nothing in excess." (The opposite pediment stated, "Know thyself.")

SPECIFICS

ALCOHOL

Moderation is particularly important when alcohol is concerned. I can think of one immortal tenor whose career was lamentably cut short by alcoholism and another who died of a broken neck in a fall induced by excess drinking. In moderation, drinking is acceptable for the singer, provided it is not done immediately before a performance to fortify the nerves. Red wine in moderation particularly is known to have a salutary effect upon the body.

TOBACCO

Tobacco and singing do not mix. If its expense, its smell, its social stigma, and its ruination of health are not enough to convince you to stop or never to start using tobacco, let singing be the reason. When I studied at Indiana University's School of Music, approximately 250 graduates and undergraduates were vocal majors. I only ever saw two among them, both males, smoking, and one already had telltale vocal signs of his habit that were sure to worsen over time.

COFFEE AND TEA

Neither coffee nor tea seems to have any adverse effects on the singing voice. Naturally, if the caffeine has not been removed, too much of these drinks jangles the nerves and may help to unbalance the singer. Too much of any liquid may prove a problem if taken within a few hours of performance, as natural nervous energy tends to tighten muscles around the bladder and heighten the need to urinate. Because caffeine also promotes elimination of excess liquid from your body, you may find yourself discomforted on the stage by a problem that could have been avoided.

DAIRY PRODUCTS

If you expect to sing within three or four hours, do not consume liquid or semiliquid dairy products or anything else that has the tendency to coat your singing passages. These produce phlegm and cloud the tone.

SINGING AND MENSES

More than a few women complain of the effect that excess fluids during menstruation have on the delicate vocal cords. This is a matter to discuss with a trusted physician. Often, the problem can temporarily be lessened with the use of a mild diuretic, although this may dry the throat.

SPEAKING

If you wish to sing well, you must protect your voice whenever you speak, because the same instrument is used for both. Never shout at athletic competitions or concerts. Don't try to compete with bands or disc jockeys at weddings and the like. Refrain from shouting in arguments, both for the sake of your voice and because there are always better ways to settle disputes.

Particularly if you find yourself speaking a great deal for your job, as schoolteachers do, or if you lecture, be sure to engage your deep breathing fully and to support your tone as you do when singing. Keep a steady stream of air flowing via the abdominal muscles so that you do not need to press down on the vocal apparatus to squeeze out sound.

Most people want to sound sexy and alluring. Therefore, they cultivate a lower sound, similar to the voices of Barry White, Cary Grant, or Lauren Bacall. This is fine if they have naturally low voices, but any attempt to force the voice lower than its normal range proves injurious over time. In fact, as a rule, it is wiser to speak a semitone or full tone higher than you normally do if you wish to keep the voice free of stress.

PREVENTIVE MAINTENANCE

Make sure to keep your teeth and gums free of disease. Oral disease is nothing to be trifled with and can result in systemic infections that can kill you. Also, once you lose your mature set of teeth, you won't get another. "Ignore your teeth and they'll go away" is more than a flip remark. I have seen up close the limitations on singers who have been forced to wear dentures.

As much as possible, make sure that the indoor places where you spend much time have sufficient humidity. Either put an inline humidifier in your home if the humidity is too low, or else purchase room humidifiers. We have several in our house that get nighttime use throughout the late fall to early spring. Ours are the cold-water mist variety. Whatever you use, make sure that they are cleaned often with a couple of drops of bleach, to prevent the growth of mold. Change the filters when recommended.

Gargling with an antiseptic mouthwash is a good practice.

Staying warm and dry is the rule during the winter. Stay out of drafts, and keep your feet warm and dry. Many singers become highly neurotic, refusing to remove scarves even indoors. However, the other extreme of pooh-poohing staying warm and dry invites colds. I have heard it stated that being cold does not gives people colds. On a superficial level, this is true. Scratching the paint off a car also does not give it rust. As long as you keep the car in a very dry garage, the exposed metal won't corrode. Similarly, if you put a person in a cold room but make sure the room is antiseptically clean, she or he won't catch cold. In real life, we can't keep cars forever in garages, and neither can we stay away from people with colds and the surfaces they touch, such as doorknobs, railings, and money. Staying warm and dry, getting enough sleep, and having a positive mental attitude all contribute to keeping one's immune system powerful.

Wash your hands often. When possible, use antibacterial soap and wash for as long as it takes you to say the alphabet. Keep your fingers away from your eyes, which may introduce as many germs as do the mouth and nose combined.

The multibillion-dollar pharmaceutical industry does not want you to know that full-spectrum sunlight is very good for you. Have you ever wondered why colds and the flu are so prevalent in the winter? Do you believe it's because germs prefer to grow in cold weather? Of course not. These germs are always around us and are as prevalent in the summer as in the winter. The difference is that when the amount of sunlight decreases and when people move indoors because the outdoors are cold, we are exposed to much less natural sunlight. The full spectrum of sunlight, when received in our eyes, stimulates the body to maintain a high level of natural defense mechanisms. In California, a health-food restaurant that installed many full-spectrum lights for its hanging plants had almost no personnel out sick with colds or flu during the winter. Similarly, a factory that produced microelectronics installed special skylights so that the workers could see better. This glass allowed in all the sun's wavelengths, and again the workers were almost totally free from colds and other respiratory infections. Full-spectrum lighting is available from catalogs and via the Internet.

ONCE YOU GET A COLD

If you merely get a cold and are suffering from sneezing, sniffles, and stuffiness, you can still sing while waiting for your body's immune system to build up and defeat the virus. In fact, professional singers sing this way all the time. Lilli Lehmann recommended starting low in the range and working upward very slowly during a cold. She used a full octave scale and the Great Scale (two octaves) (1924, 39). However, if you cannot get your sinus cavities open, if you can't stop the constant flow of mucus, or if your throat is inflamed, it is best not to sing.

One thing that will make you feel better and that will kill germs locally in the pharyngeal area is gargling with water as hot as is comfortable and highly laced with table salt. The salt kills bacteria and also draws some of the excess water from the tissues. Sniffing or atomizing saltwater up your nose also helps. It is available in a buffered form at pharmacies under the name "Ocean," but you can make it at home with dissolved table salt and preboiled water for less than a penny. Simply use an old atomizer or a nose dropper that you have boiled to kill off any other germs that might attack you while you are indisposed.

With truly bad colds and other respiratory infections that settle in the larynx, gargling will do nothing. Once the cords are infected, they usually swell a bit to protect themselves. This swelling is called *edema* and is natural. You should not sing if your cords will not respond. Stay warm, get lots of rest, drink plenty of fluids.

Lilli Lehmann shares a remedy for hoarseness:

> Pour boiling water into a saucer, and let a large sponge suck it all up [I am assuming she means a clean, new sponge that has not been used for housework or to clean the car—BJM]. Then squeeze it firmly out again. Hold the sponge to the nose and mouth, and breathe alternately through the nose and mouth, in and out. I sing my exercises, the great scale, passages, etc and all the vowels into it, and so force the hot steam to act upon the lungs, bronchial tubes, and especially on the mucous membranes. (1924, 303)

Regarding practice, many teachers and singers ascribe to what Nellie Melba wrote advising the singer with a cold: he or she should work in silence (1926, 14). Lamperti said that it is more important to learn with the head than the voice at such a time (1905, 34). Tosi, as quoted by Shakespeare, said, "Singing demands such close application, that when one can no longer practice with the voice one must study in thought" (1924, 75).

ALLERGIES

People who have allergies, either seasonal or year-round, have a definite disadvantage as singers. The first proactive step should be to reduce exposure to the offending items (these usually produce otherwise harmless proteins that the body mistakes as harmful and defends against). Those allergic to household dust shouldn't have carpeting. Those whose hands swell up if scratched by a pet shouldn't have long-haired pets. When driving during pollen season, the internal air circulation option should be used in your car; bed clothing should be sprayed against dust mites.

There are now many good products on the market that block the cell receptors that react to foreign proteins. These should be explored, preferably with a doctor's guidance. However, be aware that many of them dry out the system and make singing more uncomfortable. Others make you drowsy.

Some people benefit from scratch tests that indicate their sensitivity to various allergens. Once they know what they are most allergic to, they may work at avoidance or opt for a protracted series of desensitizing shots, administered by a physician. I know of several people, however, who had no noticeable improvement, even after years of such expensive shots.

DAMAGED VOCAL CORDS

Like arterial walls covered with plaque, unfortunately, at the present state of science and medicine, once the vocal cords are badly damaged they are never the same. Persistent wrong use or overuse of the vocal mechanism can result in permanent swellings called *nodes.* In extreme cases, these can be scraped by a surgeon. However, the cords are never again as smooth and as flexible as they once were. The best means to keep the cords healthy is never to abuse them, especially by screaming or smoking.

PHLEGM

Thickened mucus, called *phlegm,* is a nuisance in singing. It can be heard when on the cords and can cause the voice to be cloudy or even to crack. Phlegm is a natural excretion of the body, and unless it is overproduced, it must be accommodated. It can be lessened by not consuming dairy products and made thinner by drinking plenty of clear fluids. If it is persistent, this is usually an indicator of deep-seated infection, and you should see a doctor. For those with allergic or asthmatic conditions who produce too much phlegm, treatment by nasal steroid spray may produce positive results. There are also prescription medicinal thinners for mucus.

Singing in the morning is more difficult for most people because of phlegm and because the vocal cords take on a bit of water during the night. This condition normally passes after an hour or so. If you must perform early in the morning, you will do best to arise earlier.

Some singers are able to coax the phlegm off their cords by singing gently. An exercise I use is to sing in the middle of my range, repeating on the same tone over and over the sound "yum."

CLOTHING AND PERFUME

In the late nineteenth and early twentieth centuries, many singing books went on and on about clothing. Women seemed to suffer commonly from "the vapors" and fainting spells, symptoms that often had to do with corsets and other confining articles to produce exaggerated wasp waists. In general, clothing should not constrict your ability to control your breathing. This is particularly true of belts.

Regarding perfume or toilet waters, it is best not to overload when singing. Certainly, if singing with others, refrain out of common courtesy from applying scents to your person.

OVERPRACTICE

Overpractice can cause as many problems for the vocal apparatus as singing incorrectly. The muscles and ligaments of the larynx are small and delicate, like a finely made watch. You must treat them with respect. It is better by far to practice for thirty minutes at a time three times a day than for one ninety-minute session. The human body is a miraculous thing. It will generally tell you when it is being abused. In the case of vocal cords, you will feel uncomfortable at first. Then they will feel tired. Then you will hear the strain. Then they will inflame. If you persist in abusing them, they will eventually swell up so much that they no longer function.

Singers, sometimes out of desperation to earn a living or to be heard, will attempt to defeat the body's self-protection. They will go to a doctor and ask for a local cortisone shot or some steroid that will bring down swelling. This is a final and desperate act. I caution against doing this unless the doctor is a highly qualified otorhinolaryngologist who specializes in singers and their conditions and who is convinced after an internal visual examination that such action will not lead to permanent damage.

SINGING IN CHOIRS

Not a few singing teachers are opposed to their students singing with choirs. They give the reasons that students are often asked to sing too-high ranges, that they must hold back their voices for the sake of blending, that they are asked to sing things too loudly, and so forth.

In general, I do not find choral singing detrimental to my students. However, I caution them to take the director's shorthand approach to "good breathing" and "proper stance" with a grain of salt. Also, I instruct that if they are asked to sing very high or low for the sake of the pieces' rich harmonies, they should drop out or sing falsetto and let the nonserious singers do that work. They can always watch the director attentively and smile, something that is rarely done in such groups.

Singing Very Young
This is discussed in Chapter 7.

Singing Well for Years
The secret of singing well throughout a lifetime is summed up by the singer Rubini, as quoted by Salvatore Marchesi: "Sing with the interest, not the principal" (1902, 10). The wonderful coloratura soprano Joan Sutherland has been quoted more than once in repeating this adage, as has, I believe, her frequent vocal collaborator Marilyn Horne. Never push the voice. Give it rest. Learn how to sing with "no throat."

CHAPTER 7

The Teacher/The Lesson

THE TEACHER

To BEAT MY FAVORITE ANALOGY TO DEATH, an automobile needs a mechanic from time to time, to do preventive maintenance and to fix it when it breaks down. Similarly, all but the most perfect singers can benefit from objective help.

One important reason for a singing teacher is the proprioceptive hearing issue, discussed in Chapter 4. You simply cannot hear your tone quality as an outside listener can, and if that listener is skilled, so much the better. Furthermore, we all have bad habits that are so ingrained we cannot catch them ourselves. Hearing objectively and registering some bad habits can be accomplished by means of a good tape recorder and a video camera in tandem with a guide such as this one, but this is a tedious task for the would-be good singer, and it will not replace an experienced and knowledgeable teacher.

SELECTING A SINGING TEACHER

Despite the benefits of working with a teacher, I would rather you had no teacher than paid your money to and put your trust in a poor one. If my experiences are normal, there are as many poor singing teachers as good ones. The reason is that, like fortune-tellers and psychics, anyone can hang out a shingle and declare him- or herself a voice teacher; the legal system will not cart these teachers to jail for having no license from an accredited institution.

To illustrate, I once read about world-class pianist Artur Rubinstein (or was it Valdimir Horowitz?) vacationing in the summer with friends. He happened to take a constitutional walk one evening and passed a house from which piano sounds emanated. A sign near the street displayed a name and advertised that a piano teacher lived inside. The phrasing and technique were not good, and the maestro could not prevent himself from knocking on the door, introducing himself, and showing the woman what she lacked to play the piece with authority.

The next year, the great pianist was again visiting his friends and happened to stroll by the same house. Piano sounds again issued from the open windows, and they were no better than the first time. However, the sign had been appended. On the bottom, it proclaimed: "Pupil of Artur Rubinstein" (or Vladimir Horowitz).

Credentials do not necessarily guarantee good teachers. I, who have a Doctor of Musical Arts behind my name, am the first one to warn you of this. You may have had the unfortunate experience of putting your life in the hands of a physician who received a degree from an accredited university or hospital and who turned out to be seriously lacking in diagnostic abilities. The sad truth is that if a person has enough willpower, time, and money, and a bit of brains, someplace will grant him or her an MD degree. This need not be from a hospital in a banana republic, either. If it is true of medical physicians, be assured it is true of singing teachers.

Along with credentials, no matter their age, teachers should be able to demonstrate what is being taught. I do not mean that they should sound like Caruso or Lily Pons, but they should show clear evidence of vocal control and freedom. Further, they should be able to show you records of their performing experience, in terms of programs, playbills, and/or reviews. Not always, but generally, the higher the level of their experience, the more they will know about singing. One caveat here: some naturally gifted singers who studied very little have had wonderful careers, and when they became old they decided to supplement their savings by teaching. These people often have excellent professional connections for their pupils, but the pupils had better also be naturally gifted, because this class of teacher sometimes has little sound advice to offer on how to improve the singing voice. They emerged onto the singing stage like Venus appearing on Botticelli's seashell and never had to learn the rudiments. These folk will often be found at large or well-funded colleges and universities, which pay for their presence to enhance the reputation of the institution.

Many fine teachers, of course, are found working at colleges and universities. I have found that ones who were not as naturally gifted but who built their instruments and carved out careers tend to be the best teachers because of what they needed to learn to succeed. Sometimes (but not often), these people will find time to instruct singers with good potential outside their school workload. You may consider this avenue early on if you are young. If the teacher works at a college you wish to attend later, this may provide simpler ingress and in some cases could result in a scholarship.

An excellent resource for singing teachers is the National Association of Teachers of Singing (NATS), found at www.nats.org. It has more than 6,000 members, not only in the United States. A NATS member is apt to be a quality teacher because the organization has stringent membership criteria. At the time of this printing, a full member must be twenty-five years of age, adhere to a code of ethics, be recommended by a teacher already a member of the organization, be teaching at least six students per week, and have from two to five years of teaching experience depending on the level of educational experience. Logically, even these criteria do not guarantee a top-notch teacher. Moreover, even the most educated and experienced teacher may not align with your personality.

Singing teachers can advertise. That is how my parents found my first teacher. However, this is an expensive proposition for a one-on-one earning situation that is a luxury pursuit for most people and who consequently won't pay for lessons what they pay for doctors' visits. Consequently, many fine singing teachers do not use this method.

I have never advertised. All my students have come to me either because they heard me sing or because they heard my pupils sing. This is a solid resource to explore. Don't be afraid to ask a local singer you admire if she or he has studied successfully with anyone in the area.

BUYER BEWARE

I know that a temptation for many singers is to study with a teacher who is closely affiliated with an outlet for performers. This may be the high school vocal teacher who also directs or casts the school musicals, the church organist who puts on shows in the church, or the college teacher who runs an outside local theater or summer theater program. This class of teachers has been around since at least Mozart's time (as shown in the movie *Amadeus*), and many are quacks who are misusing their casting power to line their pockets. One of these creatures lived in my hometown and taught at a college. His students' lessons were almost entirely spent learning the repertoire of the shows he was putting on, both inside and outside the school. Little time was spent improving the voice or developing appropriate repertoire. If he needed a powerful singer with a very high range and didn't have one available at the time, he pushed a young soprano or tenor into the role and ruined the voice permanently without a twinge of remorse.

Everyone who studies has hopes of using his or her voice in performance. Do not, however, sacrifice long-term gains for short term gratification. Denying gratification is one of the most difficult lessons to learn in life, but it is vital in singing. If a role seems too difficult for you, it probably is.

Also beware of the singer/teacher who has had or has a career but who sings despite what she or he knows and not because of it. I studied (for reason of fulfilling credit requirements) with a naturally gifted baritone whose secret to good breath control was to push out the stomach forcefully. He would demonstrate how developed his abdominal muscles were by pushing his grand piano around his studio without using his hands. He apparently did not know that the stomach protrudes in good, deep breathing merely as consequence of the abdominal muscles being relaxed and the diaphragm above descending and compressing the soft organs of the abdominal cavity.

HOW TO SHOP

Being an educated consumer applies as much in choosing a voice teacher as in choosing a vacuum cleaner (and will produce better sounds!). Be smart and minimize risk. When you are auditioning a teacher, don't be afraid to ask questions. Certainly this book should give you plenty of material to discuss. Don't be shy about asking the teacher to demonstrate vocally. Make allowances, naturally, if the person is of advanced age. Ask teachers what their formal credentials are. Inquire who they have taught. Ask if you can have the names and contact information to be able to get third-party recommendations.

Don't be afraid to ask for a sample lesson. I have more people ask to study with me than I can handle. I invite them (and their parents if they are not at least 18) to visit me. I test their voices. If I believe they have potential, I tell them; if not, I say that, as well. I ask if they have studied with other teachers. If they have, I ask what they have learned. I speak of my methodology and of how it jibes with or differs from what they have been taught to that point. I justify my methods. I supply credentials. I demonstrate. I show them a little how I teach. I answer all questions. You should expect assurances on this order.

WHAT TO EXPECT FROM A TEACHER

Remember that singing is a psychophysical art. If you and a teacher are not aligned mentally and you don't have sufficient trust, you may not gain much.

At the opposite extreme, even if you place your trust implicitly in a teacher and the teacher is a good one, miracles may not occur. My first teacher, who in retrospect I consider my best, used to say to me, "You must think of these lessons as two friends working out a problem. Do not think I can hand you all my wisdom. I can only take you to the door; you must walk through."

Here is the same attitude described by the respected teacher Louis Arthur Russell in *Some Psychic Reflections for Singers*: "The average student leans too much upon his instructor, and is too apt to expect to be carried along by him. My advice to students is 'learn to think' and to come at once to a realization that it is *They* themselves who must do the work" (1904, 4). This is also the opinion of singer Lucrezia Bori, as imparted to Martens (1923, 3).

Buzzi-Peccia wrote, "One important point, that should be understood clearly, is that the school is the place where the student gets the IDEA which he must work out alone—at home. The improvement must come from his own mind! They [pupils] do not seem to understand that the teacher is the guide who gives them the points, but that the pupil is the one who must think them out and develop them for *himself*" (1925, 24).

Even if a teacher seems to be knowledgeable and earnestly interested in your improvement, if you find yourself hoarse after lessons or feeling tight or "uptight," you should seek out another teacher. Never study with a teacher who is not patient or who verbally abuses you. The quest to become an accomplished singer should be an exhilarating experience, with the student feeling mentally and physically better and better, more and more relaxed, balanced, and in charge.

THE TECHNICIAN AND THE COACH

There are many terms for what I am about to discuss, and consequently much misunderstanding has arisen. Just as this guide is arranged in two parts, singing teachers perform two major classes of service. The first is to help to improve the quality and handling of a voice, much as a mechanic services or improves a car's performance. This is a vocal technician. The second is to improve the singer as a musician and performer. This would be the function of the teacher at the racecar driving school. This is a coach. Often, the two can be found in one teacher. Sometimes, you will need to seek out separate persons for the two elements. I do know that all too many pianists who have sat at many voice lessons eventually believe themselves qualified to act as technicians. As good musicians, they often can talk about how a song is structured, how to phrase, how dynamics may be used, and especially how to work as a team with an accompanist. However, when it comes to the technical aspects of singing, they parrot what they have heard but can't demonstrate. They have partial knowledge and won't admit it. Beware.

THE SVENGALI TEACHER

Because you are reading this guide, there is less worry that you will fall victim to the so-called Svengali instructor. Nevertheless, I want to make you aware of this rare but harmful type of teacher. The term comes from a famous novel titled *Trilby*. Trilby was a woman who wanted to be a great singer. She was instructed by Svengali under hypnosis and improved radically. Her career took off. However, she could never free herself of Svengali, because he never told her directly how to take charge of her own voice. She was forever dependent, to her misfortune.

Some teachers do not tell the student enough simply because they don't know enough themselves. A few wish to maintain their income. They dole out hints and instruct mechanical positioning without sufficient explanation, to keep their students dependent. They constantly remind the student of their import in the process.

In the bel canto era, Italian pupils lived with their teachers for years and generally took two lessons a day. In exchange for all this speculative time and expense on the teacher's part, the student signed a contract, giving up to half his or her salary for a period of years. This no longer happens, so unscrupulous teachers instead revert to making singers mentally dependent on them. Again, beware of the teacher who is not interested in you progressing as quickly as is reasonable and in you standing on your own two feet.

THE LESSON AND OTHER CONSIDERATIONS

A TOUCH, I DO DECLARE IT

In times past, doctors in China were not allowed to ask female patients to remove any clothing or to touch them. They therefore carried nude porcelain figures, which we call "Chinese Ladies," and asked the patient to point to the area of her complaint. Imagine how difficult it would be to diagnose appendicitis!

A similar difficulty arises for singing teachers. It is often very instructive to have the student feel the difference between tight and relaxed muscles of the jaw and throat, the wrong use of the shoulder blades, the phantom "expansion" of the soft organs below the diaphragm, and so on. This would require the student to touch the teacher. Also, the teacher may benefit from feeling on the student's person the coordinations of inspiration and expiration, or the amount of air being expelled through the mouth during exercises. This is, however, a "touchy" matter. Certainly, it should not be done if the student feels uncomfortable about it. I always ask at the beginning of my relationship if this will make the pupil feel uncomfortable. For younger students, I strongly advise that the teacher have a parent attending the lessons where any touching will occur. Furthermore, even if the student is at ease with this practice, it is not something that needs to be done more than a few times, in my estimation. Of the ten persons I studied with or in whose studios I observed for a period of lessons, five invited the student to touch them, and four of these also touched the student. In every case, it took but a matter of moments and was not a common element of the lesson.

WHEN TO BEGIN TRAINING/THE YOUNG SINGER

I began training at age eleven, when I was a boy soprano. My teacher had all his life refused to train males until their voices had *mutated,* or matured. In this manner, he missed out on training the famous tenor from Trenton, New Jersey, named Richard Crooks. I think this lost opportunity, my potential, and his advanced age (therefore, little chance to teach many more pupils) led him to forgo his better judgment and work with me. I am grateful for his tutelage, but I will say that singing and studying through the change from boy to man caused me some serious although not permanent complications. Most of these arose from singing with too much intensity for someone my age, since I sang in performances.

I write this as a stern warning: There are some teachers who are heedless of any dangers to the young singer, and this has been true from at least the baroque era. Here are two opinions:

"A singer ought to be instructed at a very early period in life, and the practice ought to be gradual" (Corri 1811, 2).

Browne writes that the pupil should start "as soon as he can read" (1887, 47).

Many more teachers, however, believe as my first one did, that the immature voice can be easily damaged by overpractice, by widening the range, and by singing with too much intensity. Even though Corri believed in early training, his qualification was that it was not to be rigorous.

Because women's voices do not undergo the considerable changes of lowering an octave that men's do, coupled with the men's more pronounced hardening of cartilages, they can in general be instructed young with less fear of damage. Nonetheless, some teachers will not take any pupils until they are sixteen or older. I rarely take male students of promise earlier than their mutation, and only with the understanding that we will be working exclusively on the rudiments and working only within the range of about an octave.

Here is a sampling of what other teachers have written:

Clifton thinks that "girls can begin at 10 or 11 but not boys" (1846, 4).

Nathan writes, "Children cannot commence too soon, but men should avoid singing during mutation" (1836, 6). The singer Lablache agrees (184?, 3).

Pfeiffer and Nägeli believe girls can begin at fifteen or sixteen and boys should not do so until mutation is complete (1830, 7).

HOW LONG WILL STUDY TAKE?

As you might expect, one answer is "As long as it takes to master the skills." I would say, as a general rule, about the same amount of time that it takes to create a skilled pianist or violinist. It matters not a whit that you have already been talking and singing all your life; the truth is that until you study you have probably not been treating your voice as an instrument. What is more, if you have never studied the violin or piano, you probably have not developed bad habits of fingering and such that must be unlearned. Most singers have been singing incorrectly with great abandon for years before they study.

I have experienced persons who have apprehended the major points of vocal technique and performance in a year and assimilated them quite well. This is rare. A more usual course of study is about three or four years. Certainly, it depends on how diligently the student concentrates and how much quality time is spent practicing — that is, not merely vocalizing but doing so in a methodical fashion. I was once a student myself. The rest of life got in the way, and I was young. Often, I did not practice more than thirty total minutes between weekly lessons, and that was at the badgering of my parents (bless them).

As a graduate student, I observed a few well-established, famous singers who were far into their careers "sneaking" in and out of Indiana University's School of Music to work out some weakness that had crept into their technique or to consult on the subtleties of performing a specific piece. Even the best singer may benefit from continued or occasional study, provided it is with a trusted and highly experienced teacher.

Here is my expert backup:

Bach believes "several years under a master" are needed (1880, 11).

Botume writes, "four to seven years" (1897, 7).

Singer Emma Calvé says, "You cannot perfect a pianist or a violinist in three months and certainly not a voice" (Martens 1923, 38).

Wronski quotes the singer Rubini: "The study of our art is too long for our life. When young we have the voice but lack the schooling. Afterward, we get the schooling but lose the voice" (1921, 70).

WHAT SHOULD YOU EXPECT AT THE LESSON?

Most students take one lesson a week. The more diligent ones, or those who wish to progress more quickly, will take two or even three per week. Often, when pupils are in a musical production or preparing a recital or audition, I work with them several times in a week. Needs vary.

Lessons are highly individualized experiences. However, almost to a teacher what I experienced as pupil and observer was an initial period of technical training and, for the advanced, vocalized warm-ups. These were followed by direct application to songs and arias, either for an upcoming event or to add to repertoire.

For the beginning student, I first introduce an overview of the essential elements of good singing, then defend and demonstrate them. This takes a good deal of time. For the first three or four lessons, my students understand that they will be doing much more listening and watching than singing themselves. Many other teachers impart theory much later and spend the first weeks acclimating their students to the lesson and using just a few pointers to improve the voice little by little.

After my "break-in period," I spend ten to thirty minutes getting the student to apply technical aspects and to warm up her or his voice. This is so mentally taxing that I afterward have the student sit for a period of two to four minutes and just chat. Then we move to application of theory in songs. I begin with simple pieces, such as "Soon It's Gonna Rain," from *The Fantasticks,* or Neil Diamond's "Sweet Caroline," which allow ample time between phrases to let in breath, set, and remember to spin out the air. I ask the students if these are particular favorites of theirs. If so I don't use them, because my students work on them for so many weeks that they begin to hate them. In truth, I am using these not as songs but as an interim step, to demonstrate how the techniques we've been working on are demanded by songs and arias and to show other requirements we have not yet mastered. These early pieces give the student a concrete example of why the skill must be learned (for example, to be able to sing the phrase in one breath).

The great singer Pacchiarotti was kept on a single sheet of exercises for years. My first teacher kept me for six months on just exercises and then on the song "He" for another six months, until one day I tore it apart in frustration. Today's world is one of continuous change, and people expect to move along more quickly than they did in the baroque era or even when I began studying. My use of a few demonstrative songs is an attempt to bridge from the old style of teaching to the new.

I will admit that I also bow to pressure from singers to incorporate into their lessons music from shows, church and synagogue performances, and so on that they are engaged in. The lessons, after all, are geared to develop a skilled performer. Nevertheless, I warn my beginning students that the music is too complex for complete mastery at the time but we can always discuss the poetry, its meaning, how the composer's melodies bring it to life, how phrases should be shaded, where breaths should be let in, and other things.

For back-up, let me quote from four respected persons in the vocal world:

Corri wrote, "It is a misfortune attending our art, that songs are learned and sung before the rudiments are acquired" (1811, 2).

Myer averred that the "wrong effort is aggravated ten-fold by the too-early use of words" (1886, 17).

The professional singer Julia Clausson said to Cooke in an interview, "One of the great troubles in America is the irrepressible ambition of both teacher and pupils.... Some teachers, I am told, start in with songs at the first or second lesson, with the sad knowledge that if they do not do this they may lose the pupil to some teacher who will peddle out songs. After four or five months I was given an operatic aria; and of course, I sang it. A year of scales, exercises and solfeggios would have been far more time-saving" (1921, 96).

"When I told the maestro I wanted to learn a song he smiled and said, 'Your father is a surgeon. Ask him if, after a few days of study, he thought he could learn to perform an operation'" (Marafioti 1925, 251).

Generally, the beginner's lessons do not exceed fifty minutes. I have found over a period of years that with the level of concentration required, after this amount of time the student usually backslides. As students advance, I spend less time warming them up and reviewing technique and often go to an hour or perhaps seventy minutes, time allowing. For students practicing by themselves, I recommend thirty-minute periods. For the would-be professional, teachers generally agree not more than three sessions per day of a maximum of thirty minutes, with at least thirty minutes of rest in between.

PRACTICE, PRACTICE, PRACTICE

Remember that lessons are expensive. If you really want to improve more quickly and not to have to study forever, you need to practice diligently on your own. As in much of life, you get out what you put in.

Samuel Dilworth-Leslie, my undergraduate piano teacher and an international concert artist, would say to me, "I would rather you brought me eight perfect measures than an entire sloppy etude."

Be guided by Myers's admonition: "Practice makes perfect but it must be right practice" (1886, 17).

DOES PRACTICE MAKE PERFECT?

According to my colleague Elizabeth Strauss: "There is hardly ever an instance where singing can be said to be perfect. Rather, constantly repeated, correct 'practice makes permanent.'"

CHAPTER 8

Practice / Vocal Exercises

FIRST CONSIDERATIONS

MY WISEST TEACHER, H. ROGER NAYLOR, once wrote to me, "It is an ancient truism that we learn to do by doing. There is no royal road to knowledge. To succeed one must work, work, and work. No habit, good or bad, is formed without repetition."

Mr. Naylor was also fond of telling me that in practice, we must never say to ourselves, "Stop drawing up the shoulders" or "Stop moving the jaw forward." Even in the act of trying to undo bad habits, we reinforce them by focusing on them. He used to tell me, "You can't just get rid of a bad habit; you must replace it with a good habit." (I covered this idea at the end of Chapter 4.) He then admonished me to focus on what I must do right, to say it mentally, and to envision myself doing the thing correctly.

Remember that it is not only how many times we do vocal exercises but also how much we concentrate and bring them toward perfection.

When practicing, spend at least a bit of time in front of the mirror. It cannot be influenced by your charm and will show you with infinite patience any bad habits of breathing; tensing the neck, jaw, or lips; opening the mouth too wide; and so on.

Practice in clothing that is not constricting but that also allows observation of the three steps of breathing. Bare-midriff clothing is especially good.

Begin practice softly and increase intensity as the session goes along.

Don't be alarmed by loose phlegm coming off the cords and laryngeal and pharyngeal walls. The vibrations of singing will clear it away.

Regarding frequency: "Better one hour everyday than ten to-day and none to-morrow" (Lehmann 1924, 37).

When practicing by oneself, in general practice for thirty minutes, not more often than three times per day. This is what Manuel Garcia also recommends. If you find yourself not doing well, walk away. If you find yourself doing quite well, do not be tempted to exercise into exhaustion and lapse into old habits.

PREVOCALIC EXERCISES

Refer to Chapter 2, "Breath/The Torso," for the two standard prevocalic exercises to encourage proper diaphragmatic/intercostal inspiration "letting," followed by "setting," followed by "spinning." **Do not abandon prevocalic exercises too soon. Use them for at least a few months.** Take to heart the wise words of Louis Lablache: "We persuade the pupil to practice his breath for a long time, even without singing" (184?, 5).

Here's another quotation to back up some of your objectives in breathing: "The preliminary action in respiratory gymnastics should be to draw the shoulders backwards, and to advance the chest forwards, and upwards, by giving the spine a strong forward curve at the hinder part of the abdomen" (Holmes 1879, 166). Holmes may be a little too gymnastic in using the words *draw* and *strong,* but the images are good ones.

CRAWLING BEFORE WALKING AND RUNNING

When we first moved, we crawled. Nevertheless, we got around. Then we concentrated on the balance necessary to walk. Now we'll "get around" the notes of singing and work on the balance necessary to sing well. First we'll do it at a crawl. Then we'll learn the balance for walking and finally some jogging and running.

The past 350 years of voice teaching have produced literally thousands of exercises. There exist entire books filled with exercises and little or no instruction as to what they do or how they should be performed. There are books called *Vocalises,* which are generally complicated, lengthy exercises. I have always believed that the authors of these exercises presumed singing them alone would develop a competent singer. In my estimation, the exercises that fit on two sheets of music paper are sufficient to develop any voice, provided the student understands their purpose and how the skills developed should be applied directly to songs and arias. It is not the number of exercises but how well they are done that is important. Likewise, it is not how many times the exercises are performed but how much thought and concentration goes into each session that matters.

I have culled these exercises from many singing books. Not one of them is of my invention. Some have appeared in more than a dozen books. The messa di voce is shown and discussed in myriad books. These are, therefore, tried-and-true best sellers of the singing world. They are to the voice what the dozen or so machines in a gym are to developing the full array of strong muscles.

There is a story that when Cafferelli studied with his master, Porpora, he worked for six straight years on nothing but a single sheet of exercises. No songs, no arias. Finally, when he was sick of such discipline, he told his teacher that he believed he was ready to sing songs. His teacher agreed. Within days he was performing professionally, and within the year he was famous.

Boring as it may be, **the first three exercises only** should be done for at least a dozen practice sessions, in combination with the prevocalic exercises. If sufficient progress is not perceived, the student should persevere with just these three, returning to the first chapters of the book for pointers on the mechanics necessary before turning air into sound.

I fully understand that doing the same few exercises over and over is boring. Eventually, you feel you can do them in your sleep. This is your goal. By practicing a limited number of exercises, each of which addresses some challenge in singing a song, the singer soon does not need to think about the exercise syllables, melody, tempo, or rhythms. Therefore, she or he can concentrate on stance, elements of breathing, balance of pressure and resistance, positions of the tongue and jaw, and so on, that the exercises require. These fundamental technical demands of singing must be drilled over and over until they become habit, because the singer has no time to consider them during performance. While performing, the artist instead concentrates on interpreting the song, and because technique has been made sound through careful repetition of exercises, the singer replaces fear with confidence.

The next four exercises should be added no sooner than one more each week, never abandoning the first set. Eventually, the student should be working through all the exercises in order, never hurrying. Haste makes waste. Practice in haste; regret in leisure.

In general, the sounds of "ah" and "eh" work best for exercises. They coax open the throat, are produced in a centered part of the head, and create naturally sonorous tones. They may be preceded by any number of

97

consonants: *h* (aspirate), *s* (sibilant), *b, p, t* (plosives), *m, l, n* (liquids), *f, v* (fricatives).

The *messa di voce* and the long run exercises should not be performed until the student has good mastery and control over the first exercises. Typically, I do not use the last exercises until a year into training.

All exercises must be done in the middle of your vocal range, neither extending too high nor too low. You may be able to sing the more narrow exercises on eight to ten successive semitones. The wider the exercise, the fewer steps you will be able to practice on comfortably. All the exercises are written for a mezzo-soprano range. The baritone sings in this range but an octave lower. Baritones are often expected to use a treble clef when singing solo. In fact, all but bass soloists generally sing from treble-clef music. The tones of the exercises merely indicate the relative positions of notes. Those with high or low voices will need to transpose.

Note: The exercises are gathered on two sheets in the back of the book and may be copied for personal use only. Sung examples are given on the accompanying CD.

SINGING EXERCISES

1. PULSATED DRILLS / THE ABDOMINAL CONNECTION

The first "vocalic" exercises are called *pulsated drills*. Their purpose is not to improve tonal quality or to help the singer sing more loudly.

The point of these drills is primarily to establish the place from which the control of expiration should emanate. Second, they show the importance of maintaining resistance against the abdominal pressures by using a balancing downward chest resistance. Together, the strong muscles of the torso are demonstrated to be the source of breath control.

These drills should not be sung softly. Too *piano* will not demonstrate to the singer the feel of the abdominal muscles coming into play. Neither should they be sung loudly, or *forte,* because the tendency will be to push too hard. The objective is to use the lowest of the abdominal muscles—those where the torso connects with the legs in front—to pulse out puffs of air. These puffs must not be wasted air but should turn into firm and clear sound. An open throat will respond to much less pressure than a closed one. The student must experiment to learn how much resistance pressure is required to create a clear, medium-loud sound without it having excess (and therefore lost) air carried around it. Our Old Italian Masters would have us make tones that seem to float like boats on a sea of supported air rather than tones that sound like they're wrapped in a tonal cotton ball. Because of the balancing resistance, the abdominal muscles should not jump or push out visibly. In fact, because so great a cross-section of various stomach muscles comes into play, no single small area plays a great part; it is a subtle, concerted effort.

EXERCISE 1
Pulsated, staccato

Starting at the lowest note of his or her middle range and by repeating the exercise in ascending half-steps, the pupil sings the exercise a total of eight times, encompassing the first five tones of a scale (*doh* up to *sol*). Then the exercise is reversed (descending), singing the exercise on successively lower semitones until the original pitch is reached.

When you have practiced the sound "hah" across the entire range, switch to "ho" (like Santa's exclamation). Sing approximately two vowels per second. Other phonemes that can be used are *hay, heh, hee,* and *hoo,* each one being used exclusively for the duration of the exercise rather than the group being sung successively. The initial *h* provides a soft expulsion of air so that the vocal cords are not "stroked," or attacked hard. The vowels are the pure Italian forms, to coax sounds that resonate in the mask

Remember to use only the middle octave of your full range.

EXERCISE 1A
Pulsated three step

Next, sing up and down on three pitches, using the *h* with different vowels on successive repetitions Be sure to feel just the slightest pulsation from your lower abdominal muscles. Do not let your chest or ribs collapse or your diaphragm pop up.

This exercise is written on a minor scale; you can also try it on a major scale. You will find that minor scales are rather magically easier to sing than major ones, even though in the full octave only two or three of the tones (depending on the seventh tone) have been shifted down.

The exercise objective is to associate the propagation of tone with the low abdominal muscles doing the pulsing and the chest and rib muscles (including the back ones) resisting in the opposite direction. Note how small the actual net movement in the torso is.

After a period of weeks (not after only a few times), these exercises should be sped up, i.e. accelerated. If the abdominal muscles are indeed being used to create each staccato or marcato note and if the upper torso muscles are resisting, it should be possible to produced rapid yet clean individual tones.

Finally, the rests between each note in Exercise 1A should be eliminated, so that you are singing the exercise smoothly. When you have changed from staccato to the smooth legato, you must be sure you are still pressing with the abdominal muscles. However, now the pressure is gently continuous rather than pulsated.

Note that on both Exercises 1 and 1A, the final note is held a full four counts, or beats. Be sure to observe this, as this is your initial exercise to spin tone out smoothly from the abdominal area.

2. RESONATING IN THE MASK

This exercise is complex, but it rewards the singer with improved resonance. Singing it without thinking about it first will gain you nothing. It has three distinct parts, each fashioned to help you turn your expiration into good, high tone. The first is the "h," which is an almost inaudible start of airflow. It is initiated by your abdominal muscles and goes straight up into your *mask* (i.e., where a mask sits on the face), unimpeded in the throat. The second is the "ung," which initiates tone. It lingers on the "ng" and follows the "h" breath into the mask with a vocalized sound. If the student is singing freely and the system is open, this "ng" should vibrate the front nasal passages. Unlike many consonants and consonant combinations, "ng" can be sustained. Third and finally, a vowel follows, which replaces the "ng" in exactly the same focal point. In summation, the exercise tends to guide you into placing vowels high and forward in the head.

hung - oh,   hung - oh,   hung - oh.

EXERCISE 2
Resonating in the mask

Use variously: "h-ung-oh," "h-ung-ah," "h-ung-ay," "h-ung-ee," "h-ung-oo."

Do not rush this exercise. Stay with the "h" until you feel the flow. Continue with the "ung" until you feel the vibration in the mask. Hold on to the vowel until you feel it resonating in the mask. Each iteration should take 4 to 5 seconds. Breathe between each iteration of the "word." That is, there should be three breaths with each full exercise. The full exercise, with pauses to let in three breaths, set, and spin, should take about twenty seconds. Remember that balanced torso pressure and resistance produce high tones. Sing this exercise up and down the scale for five tones, using the different final vowel sounds.

This version simply adds a little major-third turn up and down, to see how well you can handle keeping your tone focused over several different notes.

hung - ay,   hung - ay,   hung - ay. _____

EXERCISE 2A
Plus three steps

101

3. Connecting the Tones

Exercise 3
Connecting tones

You will note that this exercise is very much like the first one, except that now the tones are legato instead of staccato — that is, connected smoothly to each other rather than disconnected. Now we focus on "spinning" the tones out. A very important lesson to learn in singing is what I call Newton's law for singing: a vocal cord at rest wants to stay at rest. When you sing, you will find that it is much easier to flow from word to word than to start and stop. This is because the cords, once stopped, must then be restarted. This takes more effort, more airflow.

With this exercise, keep the thin column of air flowing. Because of the balance of resistance from above, you will barely feel the pressure of your stomach muscles at work. This is good. If you do feel the pressure, you are probably pushing too hard and wasting air. You will then hear air that has not been made into tone escaping, the so-called "breathy tone." Remember that air pressure and not air volume is what is needed to make tone — in effect, to make the cords vibrate. If you have healthy lungs and cannot make it to the end of the exercise in one breath, you are wasting breath and not balancing pressure and resistance. Watch your chest in the mirror as you sing. Is it immediately falling? Then you are not locking the muscles of inspiration in place, to create resistance.

We use two phonemes in this exercise, changing the shape of the mouth and lips. We do not need to adjust the lower jaw for this. Do this easily, so that the focus of tone does not slip from your mask area. Even though you are constantly changing from "yah" to "no," strive to keep the phonemes connected, smooth, and at the same volume, which should not be too soft or too loud.

Note that the normal American way of saying "you" makes the initial "y" in the throat. Whenever we say "y" in good singing, we must make a *quality vowel modification,* which means to replace it with the nearest vowel or vowels that sound better. In this case, we say "ee-ah." This is a "y" made in the mask. "You" should be said "ee-oo."

Once you have mastered "Yah-no," move on to the tougher "Yah-knew" (noo). Resist dropping the "knew" into the throat. Keep up the breath flow and maintain focus. Sing this exercise eight times, up and down by semitones stepwise in the range of a fifth (first five tones of the scale). Hold the last tone four beats.

EXERCISE 3A
Disjunct tones

We use the same phonemes and now jump back and forth the distance of a perfect fourth. Do not lessen breath pressure singing the "lower" tone. Also, maintain your basic jaw position. Just because we jump a distance does not mean we make large-scale changes in breath pressure or jaw position. Practice on four semitones.

EXERCISE 3B
Adding legato steps

We tack on a stepwise movement up and down a major third. Practice on three semitones.

4. OPEN TONES

This is a simple exercise, which should be sung only with "ah" or "eh." Each measure should take about two to three seconds, so the entire exercise lasts six to nine seconds. Note that you say the phoneme three times on one breath and that you crescendo (get smoothly louder) into the second and decrescendo (get smoothly softer) into the last tone. As you articulate the second and third phonemes, you will feel a semipulse from your abdominal muscles, and you will probably also feel a gentle hitch in your larynx. Make sure this "stroke" is smooth and gentle, with only the minutest halt in the breath flow.

This exercise is so uncomplicated once mastered that you should be able during it to look in the mirror and check that your throat is loose and free, your jaw hangs open relaxed and is not thrusting forward and does not move during the exercise. your mouth opening is not too wide, your lips are relaxed, and your eyes and cheeks are free of rigidity. The objective is to spin out the tones on a steady but fine stream of breath that is barely interrupted, turning all the air into tone, and sending it high and forward.

Repeat this exercise on seven semitone levels with "ah" and then come back down the same steps with "eh."

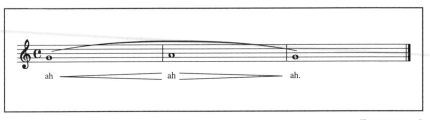

EXERCISE 4
Open tones

5. FREE MOVEMENT OF THE LIPS AND TONGUE

EXERCISE 5
Free tongue and lips

This is one of the most cited old Italian exercises and should be done with pure Italian vowels. The tongue, lips, and jaw are herein challenged by a constant change of vowel and consonant. There are two skills to master here: the first is never to "hit" these consonants hard but to say them as softly as possible. Think of how Italians speak, how the consonants roll off their tongues rather than being chopped and spat out. For example, when making the "m," don't purse your lips by pressing them together hard. Rather, simply close the lips easily for an instant. With the "p," say it as you would "pajama" and not "pop." The second skill is to merely "tip" the consonant in between a steadily flowing set of vowels. You may first wish to sing the exercise without the consonants, as "ah-eh-ih-oh-oo-ah-ehy." Then see just how little you can interrupt the same sounds with the consonants placed in between.

Actually, the Italians wrote this exercise as "da, me, ni, po, tu, la, be." I have phoneticized it as closely as English will allow. Strive to focus each of these in front of the upper teeth and maintain uninterrupted abdominal pressure as you say them, and you will match the Italian vowels.

The purpose of this exercise is twofold. The first goal is to sing legato despite the interpolation of consonants (because we must eventually use them in words). The second is to move from vowel to vowel but always to keep the vowels high and resonating in the mask with breath pressure and open throat.

6. DIFFERENT VOWELS/SAME FOCUS

me   may   mah   mow   moo.

EXERCISE 6
Pure, high vowels

This exercise, also old, compels the singer to move from the wide extreme of the mouth to the narrow one in vowel making. This must be done smoothly and easily, with no tensing.

EXERCISE 6A
Pure vowels, reverse order

This is the reverse of Exercise 6, moving from rounded to wide lips. The exact order of vowels probably came about through trial and error, but it is now tried-and-true. First use "m," followed by "n," "b," "l," and finally "t." Note how the "t" works against the legato flow from one vowel to the next, but you can still keep up breath flow and pressure if you concentrate.

7. AGILITY

EXERCISE 7
Agility

If you support your breath and if your tongue is not serving double duty also holding back your breath, the tip should be able to sing this exercise quite rapidly. This acts as a barometer for support and lingual freedom. Once you begin to get the coordination of lowering the diaphragm, expanding and then setting the ribs, you should be able to repeat this exercise five or six times freely. You can do this on the same pitches or go up and down the scale.

8. THE MESSA DI VOCE

The Italian phrase messa di voce translates as "modulation of the voice." I smilingly refer to it with my students, after they have tried it and complained about lack of success, as "the *dreaded* messa di voce." This is the quintessential

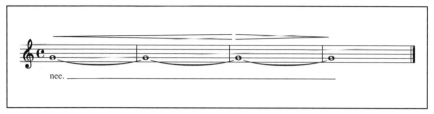

EXERCISE 8
Messa di voce

bel canto exercise. It has been analyzed and discussed ad nauseam, but it is always spoken of with reverence. It is the unfailing barometer of whether or not a singer is truly mastering breath control. It requires the smoothest and steadiest increase of tone from *pp* to *ff*, followed by a mirror-image decrease from *fortissimo* to *pianissimo*. Here is what the great Lamperti writes:

> The diaphragm must work easily and elastically, like India rubber, letting the air stream out gently. The *Messa di voce* is produced solely by breath-control. The spinning out of the tone (*filare la voce*) is very difficult; it must be managed with the utmost circumspection. (1905, 21)

According to Shakespeare, Lamperti asserts in his *Treatise on the Art of Singing* that

> we are better able to steady the breath when the lungs contain a supply for singing eighteen seconds at the commencement of a phrase, than when they are only half filled with a capacity for singing ten seconds or less; in other words, all our singing should be done on a breath-reserve of between twenty seconds or more plus five seconds, *and we should always have this latter quantity in reserve at the close of the phrase.* (1898, 16)

Many of my students begin with twelve or thirteen seconds of capacity on what they suppose is a full breath. (I usually test them after four or five lessons, specifically to show them their lack of respiratory coordination and to give them a tangible goal. I demonstrate that it can be done. Then I do not return to it again for months.) Within six months, most students can sing the messa di voce for twenty to twenty-three seconds. After two years, several have had thirty seconds or more of tone-spinning capacity, with the finest shading of crescendo and diminuendo and without exhausting their lungs.

There are two necessities for mastering this exercise. The first is to relax the abdominal muscles enough so that the diaphragm can truly lower to a flat position and so the lungs can be deeply filled. To exceed twenty seconds, intercostal breathing must be added to pure diaphragmatic lowering. The second necessity is to balance upward pressure and downward resistance perfectly while keeping the throat and head truly open, so that the tiniest filament of air can create tone. There must also be absolutely no escaping of unvocalized air, which requires the student by practice to know just how much air will create tone for each degree of intensity.

I advise the student to think about filling the lungs in the back as well as the front to create another two or three seconds of tone. I tell them that a small trick is to begin the instant the lungs are filled and the diaphragm is set, not pausing to think and consuming air for life.

Everyone can eke out a final two seconds by overexhausting the lungs (about 40 percent of the capacity of the lungs is not normally expelled unless the lungs are collapsed, and this is known as *residual air*), but I stop the student as soon as I hear this, because the next breath is sure to be drawn or "taken," and not let in, under such stressful circumstances. **A singer must never use his or her air to exhaustion,** and this exercise is as good a place to drill this in as any.

9. Agility and Smoothness

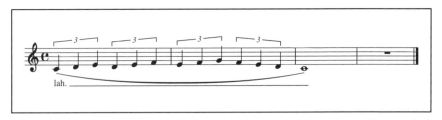

EXERCISE 9
Agility and smoothness

Once good control is attained, we begin to work on range, agility, smoothness, and duration. This is the first of such exercises. With this exercise, we begin to exceed the comfortable middle octave of the singer's range. Little by little, the scale can be climbed to explore the ability to sing higher notes without cracking, tightening, changing into falsetto, or using a breathy, unsupported tone.

The mechanics of singing high are precisely the same as those for singing in the middle range. The only difference is in degree. Because the air must be pressurized to move tauter vocal cords, the balancing resistance must be more secure. Many accomplished singers feel this upper tone resistance most in the middle to lower back. This exercise is a particularly good way to begin exploring your upper range, because for some reason the smooth rises and short falls make approaching higher notes far easier than jumping up to them. I often work my students up an extra semitone or two with this exercise and then show them on the piano where they have gone. They are amazed at how easy it was. Later, when they must hit the same notes in a song and they are looking at the music, they will revert to throaty or breathy singing because they "know" they can't hit such high notes.

Once the perfect mechanics of breath and support are mastered, the only limitations on the high end are those natural ones of the vocal cords.

Do not rush this exercise when you first approach it.

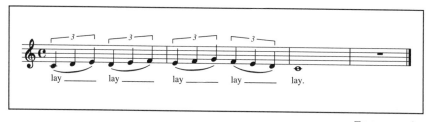

EXERCISE 9A
With more articulation

Sing the first modification of the exercise with "lah," "lay," "loo," and "lee." With this also, use several vowels in succession. This time you will repeat the phoneme with each triplet. However, keep the breath flowing, and hold the final note.

EXERCISE 9B
Smooth and detached

This modification both expands the exercise and requires legato and staccato singing (i.e., smooth followed by detached). Make sure you hold the last note the full four beats. If this is not possible with one breath, return to your prevocalic and early exercises.

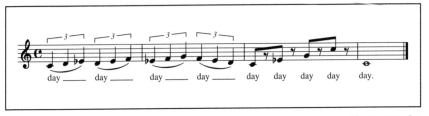

EXERCISE 9C
Full octave

Now we make our first approach to a full octave. Note that I have written this in the minor mode to make it easier. Begin this exercise with your lowest note that is easy to sing and don't move up more than three or four semitones. If you wish, you may change the exercise to the major mode.

10. THE FULL OCTAVE

Not all songs have only *conjunct* or stepwise motion. Most have some disjunct jumps. These jumps often occur toward the end of the piece, when you may be mentally or physically tired and when full-voiced singing is demanded. If you are singing "Over the Rainbow," you will be required to make a full octave leap on your first two notes. This exercise begins to prepare you for such movement. Use stepwise practice up and down a range of a fifth.

EXERCISE 10
Octave legato, fifth staccato

Now add the staccato notes up the tonic (first scale note) chord to the full octave.

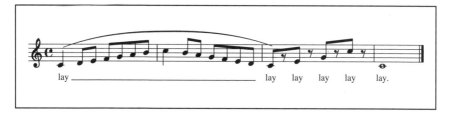

EXERCISE 10A
Octave legato and staccato

11. MORE OCTAVE LEAPING

This exercise requires the big jump from the very first. It is best to think the top note before beginning and set your resistance accordingly. Note that the syllables change.

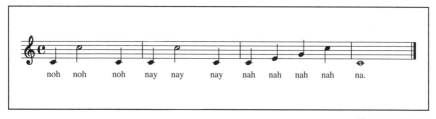

EXERCISE 11
Octave leaping

Here is a slightly altered form of the exercise, requiring quicker changes of phonemes.

EXERCISE 11A
Articulation

111

12. EXTENDING THE LINE

With this exercise, we sing an unhurried line of wavering tones finished by the octave jump. Be sure you stay on the pitches and do not go flat.

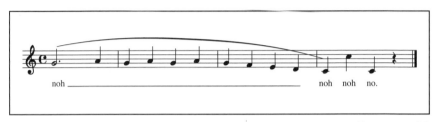

EXERCISE 12
Extending the line

13. INCREASING AGILITY

Each group of four eighth-notes should be sung in a second or less, but each should also be cleanly articulated, so that all the notes can be heard and have equal value. Use various vowel sounds and work up and down a major third. Renew breath as quickly as you can do it correctly, and sing numerous times without pause.

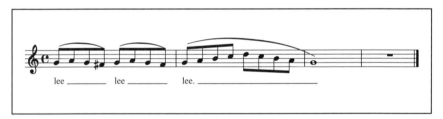

EXERCISE 13
Increasing agility

OTHER CONSIDERATIONS

WORKING ON THE LOW END OF THE RANGE

Singing in the low end of your voice is relatively easy. The emphasis here, unlike in the rest of your range, is to use more air. The cords are thick and sluggish and must have more molecules blowing across to move them. Therefore, in singing low, the singer must remember to accommodate by larger or more frequent breaths. Do not, however, produce a breathy sound; this air must also be supported and not wasted.

There is a dangerous tendency in singers to make low notes louder by pressing down on the larynx from above. This is not a good practice. It usually does little damage when the cords are not taut, but it reinforces a bad habit that must not be extended into the normal and high ranges. Further, it usually sounds throaty and not united with the rest of a singer's tones, and therefore is not appreciated by listeners. It is far better to push more air past the cords and to be content that the sounds made at the bottom of the range will not be loud or brilliantly ringing.

Exercises 1, 3, 4, and 5 are good for practicing in the low range of the voice.

ASSIMILATING GOOD HABITS

As a singer progresses, she or he must spend less and less time thinking about the mechanics of good singing and more and more on musicianship and performance. Therefore, natural assimilation of everything discussed in the book to this point must take place. I call it "moving the facts from the front of the brain to the back." By this I mean making it automatic and subconscious.

For this to happen, incorporating every aspect of good singing, "overnight" is too much to expect. Singers may assimilate several elements at a time and take "one step backward for every two forward," or else they begin to coalesce related groups of thoughts together into a *gestalt* (i.e., a complex structure considered as a whole). Here is my suggestion for how to approach total assimilation:

Stance and Inspiration — Gestalt Checklist

BEGINNER	INTERMEDIATE	ADVANCED
weight on front foot		
buttocks firm and forward	weight forward	
convex spine		
high chest	military position	"proud position"
shoulders low and back		
low blades	shoulder blades	
horizontal head		
throat relaxed and low	no throat	no throat

unhinged jaw	unhinge	
high back tongue	Cinderella's slipper	sneeze/yawn
low front tongue		
relaxed cheeks		

free abdomen	diaphragmatic/intercostal	breathe down and out
descending diaphragm		
expanding ribs		

The student should capture a complete image of singing well, both in a physical state and in an inner sensory fashion. Eventually, it is hoped, even this will not be needed.

PART II

The Artistry of Singing

CHAPTER 9

Musicianship

ONE CAN NO MORE BECOME AN ACCOMPLISHED SINGER without learning the rudiments of musicianship than one can be a novelist without learning to read or without reading good books.

ESSENTIALS

LISTENING

In my estimation, sound musicianship begins with listening to good musicians. This does not mean that you have to fill your ears every day with Puccini and Schubert, sung by Mirella Freni or Dietrich Fischer-Dieskau. I would, however, caution young singers to rely more on the sounds of performers from several decades past or at least those who perform composers from several decades past, because time has a way of burying the poor musicians and composers who may be more a product of hype, fad, and packaging than talent and application. You must cultivate the emulation of the best performers if you want to put yourself among their number. Remember that I say emulation, and not slavish duplication. You must always retain your own style and taste.

For my money, the early recordings of Frank Sinatra and Barbra Streisand cannot be beaten among mainstream singers. Two fine popular baritones are Robert Goulet and Josh Groban. A wonderful bass-baritone is the Broadway singer Brian Stokes Mitchell. The works of Celine Dion and Vanessa Williams, and the early recordings of Whitney Houston, are in my estimation worthy of emulation. There are many, many more fine popular singers.

Do not think that I'm convinced there are no excellent jazz, blues, country-and-western, or rock singers. There are many. The famous French composer Hector Berlioz was also one of the most influential music critics in the Paris of his time. He said something to the effect that "Individually, members of an audience may be imbeciles, but collectively an audience is infallible." I mention this because it is rare to have vocal soloists maintain successful careers without also having a refined sense of style and either a fine natural voice or one that is trained (the exception being those artists who are far better composers than singers and who live by the strength of their compositions).

Listening to the singers I listed here will give you a sense of what good placement and resonance are, what good breath control and phrasing mean, and how to craft a song to bring its intent to full meaning. Among classical singers, you will spend your time wisely if you listen to the likes of Ezio Pinza, Lawrence Tibbett, Leonard Warren, Boris Christoff, Nicolai Ghiaurov, Bryn Terfel, Robert Merrill, Jussi Bjoerling, Nicolai Gedda, Placido Domingo, Luciano Pavarotti, Frederica von Stade, Jessye Norman, Eileen Farrell, Kirsten Flagstad, Victoria de los Angeles, Leontyne Price, Elizabeth Schwarzkopf, Kiri Te Kanawa, Mirella Freni, and Lily Pons. These great artists are my particular favorites, and there are dozens more.

Unless you are an established and sought-after vocal star, people are not going to come to you with music to perform; you will have to seek it out. That means you will also need to listen to many composers and composer-performers. Even if you write your own music, you must be knowledgeable of various styles in order to know how to conform to and break rules successfully, and this requires extensive exposure by listening.

READING MUSIC

Never mind that the Beatles couldn't read music; they are the exception to the rule. Anyone who aspires to be an accomplished performer must be able to read music. This skill is critical in working with other musicians. It is especially important if you ever expect to be performing new works, either as a recording artist or in shows. Other musicians do not wish to tolerate having to wait while they or someone else pound the correct notes and rhythms into your head. You will be looked upon with disdain among those you want to have as peers.

If you haven't begun in school with reading music, the "international language" is not very difficult. The thing to do is to get the printed music sheets or scores of songs or shows you like and follow along until the notes and the sounds align. This is probably how you learned to read: you looked at the book while your mother or father read to you, until you associated the words with the sounds.

Learning to play an instrument is not only an excellent way to learn to read music, but it may also supply you with accompaniment. The guitar and the piano are the two most common means of accompaniment, with the piano being the more versatile.

Sight reading is, no surprise here, the ability to pick up music and read it on sight. Music schools and conservatories generally offer and often require that singers take a sight-reading course. Although this kind of immersion in reading music is beneficial for saving time, I personally believe that many other aspects of musicianship take higher priority. The number of occasions on which I have been required to sing a piece cold in a performance setting I can count on one hand and have fingers left over. Also, over time, the practice of making music naturally improves sight-reading. If, however, you would like to speed up the process on your own, there are books that will help you develop the skill.

APPROACHING MUSIC

All too often, when performing music that is already in vogue or in the repertoire, we think we know the composer's and librettist's intentions. However, if we truly take the time to go over the music measure by measure, we will find that many famous performers sing the wrong notes, breathe in the wrong places, and get the rhythms wrong.

A well-known example of disregard for the melody is that of Rex Harrison in *My Fair Lady.* It is clear from the cast recording that he was not tone-deaf, but when the song's range went beyond his most comfortable tones, he just plain spoke the words. His acceptance in this musical role excused a spate of later quasi–singing stars who could barely hold their own musically (and in my opinion this was one factor that helped to drive the musical audience away from Broadway in the years between 1975 and 1990).

My advice is to approach every piece of music, no matter how familiar you think you are with it, as if you had never seen it before. Work with it slowly. Play each pitch on a piano or guitar, to be sure it is the one you assume it to be. Especially count out the rhythms.

Whenever you have never heard a piece you may perform, go to the printed music first and not to recordings by artists. Learn the piece from the composer and librettist rather than secondhand. Make the piece your own. Then and only then should you refer to interpretations by others. You may indeed find that they are doing something with the piece that you want to borrow, but you will not be hampered by the sound of their interpretation in your ear from the first.

SELECTING MUSIC

If you land a role in a musical, operetta, or opera, there is no music-selection choice available to you, other than the occasional power to ask that a certain song or aria be accompanied in a different key. Requests for key changes are sometimes accommodated in classical music because a phenomenon called *scordatura* came about during a period of more than 100 years, with orchestral string players seeking a brighter sound by playing ever so slightly higher. Now the Queen of the Night in *The Magic Flute* is singing a double-high F about a full tone higher than when Mozart wrote it.

If you are not performing a set collection of music, you need to assemble pieces, either of your own creation or those of others, into what is called your *repertoire*. Eventually, you will settle on pieces you really like. They will become your standards, which are often called *old warhorses* or *chestnuts*.

A good way to select popular music is by listening to recordings or attending performances. A second approach is to listen to the radio, including the oldies stations. Another is to borrow recordings or videotapes from a library that has music. A fourth method is to visit a good music store and pore over their sheet music, anthologies, scores, and such.

For the classical singer, there are books that list repertoire for different vocal timbres and ranges. One old standard is Sergius Kagen's *Music for the Voice* (Bloomington, IN: Indiana University Press, 1968 [first printing]). Some online sources for music can be found at www.halleonard.com, www. colonymusic.com, www.jwpepper.com, www.patelsons.com, www.schirmer. com, and www.musicnotes.com, which at this printing has a service that will transpose music into your key of choice.

KNOW THYSELF

For every vocal range and every personality, there is a corpus of music that serves best. Some people with Carmen Miranda, Martha Raye, or Danny Kaye zany-type personalities are not meant to sing languid love songs. Alternately, Bing Crosby and Joan Sutherland were not cut out to sing low comedy. It seems that every bass wants to sing a few tenor pieces, and every alto wants to sing things for the soprano repertoire, and vice versa. Some songs work in many keys; many do not. For example, "The Impossible Dream" from *Man of La Mancha* or "Stars" from *Les Misérables* are for a bass-baritone or a baritone. They don't work for tenors or for women. If your voice is heavy and you have trouble singing quick syllables, do not attempt "I'm Not Getting Married Today" from Stephen Sondheim's *Company* or Gilbert and Sullivan patter songs. Listen to singers who seem to have vocal weight, agility, and personalities similar to yours and see what sort of repertoire they have cultivated.

CHAPTER 10

Pronunciation and Diction

A tone is a flower of the lips.
— OLD ITALIAN MASTER SAYING

VOLUMES HAVE BEEN WRITTEN about correct pronunciation in singing, particularly aimed at the singer who is performing works in foreign languages. This little guide will not go into the minutiae of the whys and hows of pronunciation, and it will address only neutral American English such as is cultivated by television anchorpersons. It is true that vowels and consonants are not always produced precisely the same way in singing as in speaking, because singing extends vowels and consonants and often expresses them across a range of intensities. Nevertheless, even the untrained singer knows many of these modifications instinctively.

VOWELS

In singing, vowels are grouped into several classes. Vowel groups include the following:

1. Closed vowels, "oh," "ooh," "uh," and "ur." They are produced, as you can feel, back in the head and in the throat. When you produce them, you can feel the throat and tongue lowering and the soft palate rising.

2. Frontals are "ee" (high), "eh" (midfront), "a" as in *lamb* (low front), and "ah" (low central).

3 Open vowels are "ih," "eh," "a" as in *sat*, and "ah" as in *father*.

It is enough for most singers to be aware of the vowel groups. The main reason to know that there are so many vowel forms and to understand whence they emanate is to be able to modify them and still maintain intelligibility.

PURE VOWELS

We already know that we sing primarily on vowels. "A, e, i, o, u, and sometimes y" were not picked arbitrarily from the alphabet and appointed to serve as the carrying sounds. Vowels came long before the alphabet was even conceived or before sounds were divided into vowels and consonants. (I believe it was Ambrose Bierce who called the alphabet something like "an arbitrary set of symbols placed in arbitrary order.") Vowels are the group of sounds that we can keep going virtually as long as we have breath — in effect, they are the main carrying sounds. We can sustain certain liquid and fricative consonants, such as "l," "m," and "v," but they carry less well.

In general, there is little that delights the musical ear as much as a pure vowel sung high in the mask. **Strive to use the pure Italian "ah," "eh," "ih," "oh," and "oo" whenever doing so makes intelligible sense to your listener. Remember that the best aid to good tone and diction is pressurized air lifting the tones into the head's resonating chambers.**

DIPTHONGS

English is one of the richest languages in the world, both in the extent of its vocabulary and in the variety of sounds that make up words. This is because English is a hybrid language, made up of Frisian, German, Angle, Saxon, Celt, Norman, Latin, and several other languages. One of the legacies of this mixing is *diphthongs*, or combined vowel sounds that we tend to think of as one. When we say the American English vowel group, we usually say, "A-ee, Ee, AH-ee, OH-oo, ee-OO." The second of the sounds for *a, i,* and *o* is called the *vanish* or the *vanishing element*.

As a general rule when singing in English, you should hold the first vowel of the diphthong as long as you can and then add the second at the last moment. The human ear wants to hear a prettier, rounder, open sound, rather than a closed or wide sound. Listeners pick up almost as much intelligibility in sentences from the context and structure as they do from the words themselves. They are also accustomed to filling in parts of words and to waiting for the final elements. Therefore, it doesn't matter to the listener if we sing "If he walked into my life toda-------y" (from *Mame*). If we rush to the "y" and hold it for four or five beats, we sound at best like we're in pain and at worst as if we're calling pigs.

MODIFYING AND SUBSTITUTING VOWELS

There are four reasons in singing to modify vowels. The first is if the vowel is one that is made too far back in the head or low in throat. An excellent example of this is the oft-used word *love*. Even though we spell the word with an *o*, we pronounce it with a guttural "uh." Now, we do not want to substitute some vowel that alters the sound of the word so much that it is either difficult to understand or just plain sounds wrong. We know that the Italian "oh" is much too high. If we sing "lohve," we sound silly or affected. However, we can color the normal "uh" with some "oh" and split the difference. The resultant sung "love" resonates higher in the head and actually sounds more pleasing to the listener.

The second reason for modifying vowels is if the singer deems that the sound is too "wide" or "white." In such cases, vowels are modified backward into the mouth by raising the soft palate and lowering the tongue and jaw a bit.

Vowels must also be modified when intensity or volume increases. The physics of sound dictates that the resonating system must enlarge to accomplish this modification. Enlarging alters the vowel sound and sometimes the phoneme (the smallest unit of language that conveys meaning), such as "er" or "bee." To compensate, the singer engages in *vowel modification* and *phonemic migration*. These big words are not to be taken too seriously, because the singer controls this modification via auditory feedback. Within a fraction of a second, the ear knows if the vowel or phoneme will be unintelligible to the listener and adjusts it accordingly.

The fourth reason to modify vowels is simply that certain vowels cannot be made in the higher reaches of the female voices. For example, *i* has a first formant frequency (ca. 300 cps) lower than the fundamental tone of many pitches females sing. Again, the nearest vowel with resonance should be selected.

CONSONANTS

We sing on the vowels; we make sense of the words with the consonants. Did you know that we are not sure if the celebrated ancient Egyptian princess's name was Nofrett, Nefertiti, or Nefretiti? That's because in hieroglyphics, even though there were vowel notations, commonly only the consonants were used. This practice may seem short-sighted on the ancient Egyptians' part, and I'm sure it must have caused some confusion every now and then with words of similar consonants and different vowels. However, to see just how relatively more important consonants are than vowels in transferring intelligibility, consider this sentence: "Wht hth Gd wrght?"

Even if you have never heard of this sentence as the first one ever used in a telegraph transmission in the United States, you might well have been able to figure out that it means "What hath God wrought?" And this sentence contains two words that have dropped from everyday usage!

In singing, a little consonant goes a long way. Therefore, we use consonants as van Gogh used the shade black, to outline and give an edge to the shapes given body with his brilliant colors. Particularly if we are singing legato (smooth) lines such as in ballads, we should strive to sing from vowel to vowel with only a bit of consonant in between. For example, "When I fall in love / It will be forever" is sung thus:

"Whe-----nI---efaw----lli--nlo------ve /
I-----twill---be fo---reh---vuh---r."

This approach does not work, however, when singing humorous or "up-tunes." For example, the Gershwin song "They All Laughed" is sung rather quickly. Therefore, only the last word can extend the vowel or vowels. "Luck Be a Lady Tonight," from the musical *Guys and Dolls*, is another example. With such songs, it is more important to emphasize the consonants and to enunciate them clearly; otherwise, the audience will not be able to apprehend them because of the song's quick tempo. Nevertheless, the song will sound better if the singer feeds a steady column of air using the abdominal muscles, just as with legato singing.

In Gilbert and Sullivan's "Model of a Modern Major-General" from *The Pirates of Penzance,* and other so-called patter songs; in Rossini's "Largo al Factotum" from *Il Barbieri di Siviglia;* in Stephen Sondheim's "Now" from *A Little Night Music;* in "Not Getting Married Today" from *Company;* and in others of this ilk, the consonants must actually be clipped and tapped lightly as one would do using a tack hammer, in order to make them sound clearly.

FORMING CONSONANTS

One error of the uneducated singer is to use too much force to form a consonant. The lips do not need to be pressed together to form an "m"; they simply need to be closed. The tongue does not need to press hard against the back of the upper teeth to form an "l." It needs only be in that position. The less effort made in forming consonants, the easier it is to release them and glide to the next vowel or consonant.

FINAL CONSONANTS

If you attend choral concerts, one way you can tell if the choirmaster is attentive to detail is whether you can hear the final consonants in words, especially "d" and "t." Failure to attach the final consonant most often arises when a word is held long. Generally, final consonants should not be struck hard, but they should be sounded.

I have not said much about this subject because it is simple and self-evident. Rest assured, however, that this is one of the most common failings of pupils, particularly with the last word of a phrase whose vowel is held for several beats. The audience will be quite confused if you want them to hear "I feel great!" but you sing, "I feel gray."

INITIAL SOUNDS

USING CONSONANTS TO TEST THE WATER

Over the years, I have observed my students using a softly made "m," "n," or "l" that in fact is not in the first word, to test whether they are about to begin a phrase on the correct pitch. It is a subtle thing, but it is nonetheless audible, and this crutch should not be imposed on the audience. What is amazing is that the singer's test sound is generally true to the intended pitch and therefore unnecessary. It is a mark of the singer's lack of confidence in her or his ability to hit the correct pitch from silence. Once I bring this habit to the student's attention (often over and over), it can be eliminated.

I am not the only teacher who has experienced this phenomenon. Lablache wrote, "We must avoid commencing a sound, by preceding with a kind of preparation, which may be expressed by *um*" (184?, 5).

SCOOPING

There is another class of singer with a problem beginning phrases. These singers are not at all unconfident of their first tone and have no qualms about entering as much as a minor third lower than the target pitch and *scooping* up. A bass-baritone who had sterling careers at the Metropolitan Opera and Covent Garden, and who created a starring role in at least one famous opera and one musical, had this habit. His natural talents and acting abilities compensated, but his scooping habit was noted with disfavor by other singers and by conductors.

Some early radio-era crooners cultivated scooping as an affectation. Judy Garland's immortal rendition of "Over the Rainbow" is rife with scooping. The Andrews Sisters even did it as a trio. At the time of this printing, scooping is not in vogue. I view it as a habit that can usually be corrected simply by drawing the student's attention to it.

To be sure, no singer can hit every note right on target, and recordings can prove that we are constantly singing and adjusting to target pitches with a natural ear-to-throat compensatory process called the *autonomic servo-system*. This, however, does not excuse sloppy singing in terms of approximating pitches.

ASPIRATING

Another habit is *aspirating*, or preceding the initial tone with unvocalized or barely vocalized air. When done unconsciously, it is a product of poor management of the balance of pressure and resistance in the strong muscles of the torso.

Shakespeare recommends aspirating as a technique to be cultivated and would have singers sing as if they were always doing the second vocal exercise I recommend: "Do not venture to sing without aspirating the word about to be sung, as though *warming* some object" (1910, 54).

Some teachers also recommended aspirating as an improvement over beginning phrases with a hard attack, called the *coup de glotte* (see the following section). If aspirating is cultivated, at the very least the air allowed to escape will limit the length of phrases that the performer can sing and will necessitate the letting in of more breaths.

THE CLEAN ATTACK

I personally do not like using the word *attack* in teaching singing, because good singing should be effortless, and attacking conjures a violent image. However, each phrase in singing must be started cleanly. This clean start is not achieved by tightening the throat or bearing down on it against the breath pressure. It is done by diligent practice, until you know instinctively how much pressure with each type of vowel or consonant and on varying pitches is necessary to start without a hard hit, scooping, breaking, or breathiness.

In the nineteenth century, something called the *coup de glotte* was recommended for a clean beginning to a phrase. If this sounds like *coup d'état*, you are right. It is the recommendation of an actual conscious closing of the cords so that the rising air pressure strikes them suddenly open and means, in effect, the "stroke of the glottis." This practice has gone out of fashion.

MASTER THOUGHTS ON INITIAL SOUNDS

D'Aubigny wrote about the clean initial attack in 1803. In 1857, Bassini wrote, "The point is, to attack the given sound, previously in mind, with precision and confidence…. The attack *must be direct and instantaneous*" (5).

Van Broekhoven declares that "the attack should be softened with the thought of an aspirate H" (1908, 21). Note that he recommends thought and not action. What he wants is a gentle entrance to each phrase rather than a shock.

The high-water mark of the *coup de glotte* theory is Garcia's adoption. In his 1894 book, he writes:

Q. What do you mean by the "stroke of the glottis?"
A. The neat articulation of the glottis that gives a precise and clean start to a sound.

Q. How do you acquire that articulation?
A. By imitation, which is quickest of all; but in the absence of a model, let it be remembered that by slightly coughing, we become conscious of the existence and position of the glottis, and also of its shutting and opening action. The stroke of the glottis is somewhat similar to the cough, though differing essentially in that it needs only the delicate action of the lips and not the impulse of the air. The lightness of the movement is considerably facilitated if it be tried with the mouth shut. Once understood, it may be used with the mouth open on any vowel. The object of this is that at the start sounds should be free from the defect of slurring up to a note or the noise of breathing. (1894, 13–14)

Certainly, Garcia's desire that slurring up and breathiness be eliminated is laudatory. Some singing experts who agree with him include Marchesi, Daniell, Myer, Curtis, Russell, Bach, Miller, and Botume. However, real opposition to the technique appears around 1900 and includes many detractors, such as Lamperti: "The injurious 'stroke of the glottis' should under no consideration be employed in tone-attack; it ruins the voice, and ought, in spite of the apparent certainty attained in tone-production, to be wholly eschewed" (1905, ion). Some other detractors were Caruso, Lankow, Shaw, Duff, Hulbert, and Melba. Anna Lankow in fact was a collaborator of Garcia's, but she rejected the attack as "a kind of shock" that might cause "diseases of the cords, such as nodes or knots of the same" (1903, 19).

JOINING THE NOTES

He who cannot join the notes cannot sing.

—OLD ITALIAN MASTER SAYING

Western music is notated as a succession of "eggs with stems" spread across five-line "fences." This method of notation is a sad historical accident for many singers, who see the large spaces in between the notes and subconsciously think of music that way. In reality, music is generally meant to be a continuous flow of sound. All too often, amateurs sing lines the way amateur cartoonists draw them, hatching away instead of pulling a smooth, continuous line. This practice is not only unmusical; the frequent stop and start of tones requires the vocal cords to endure numerous tiring "strokes." What is more, the stopping of the breath flow lowers the pressure that, if maintained, keeps the singer's tones resonating in the mask. The singer should be acutely aware that the look of notated music and its sound are two separate things.

I have put the following admonition, based on an idea from Shakespeare, in this chapter on pronunciation because the singer handles this flow by extending vowels as much as by maintaining breath pressure: **Think of words as pearls in a necklace touching each other, held together by a string formed of constant breath pressure beneath them** (1924, 55).

CHAPTER 11

Interpretation

UNTIL MICHELANGELO SAW IN THAT STONE the image of David and took away the unnecessary, it was just a chunk of beautiful Carrara marble. Similarly, a song may be potentially beautiful, but it needs a skilled singer to truly make it live. The art lies not only in combining beautiful tones with words but also in combining that skill with the craft of using phrasing, silences, dynamic shadings, emphases, tempo changes, body language, and the like to turn the music and words into an emotional, human experience.

ELEMENTS OF INTERPRETATION

IN THE BEGINNING IS THE WORD
If the major difference setting the singer on a higher plane than other musicians is the word in combination with the music, then we had better pay attention to the words from the very beginning. Every fine song has well-planned words behind it. They may sound like greeting card hokum without the music, but often this simplicity is intended.

According to Manuel Garcia,

> The pupil must read the words of the piece again and again till each finest shadow of meaning has been mastered. He must next recite them with perfect simplicity and self-abandonment. The accent of the truth apparent in the voice when speaking naturally is the basis of expression in singing. (1894, 59)

Clippinger agrees with Garcia:

When approaching a new song or aria, I insist that my students **read the words aloud.** They do this once **for understanding.** The next time, I ask them to put emotionality and phrasing into the reading. I ask them what the piece is about in general and what they must convey. If it has context in a poem cycle, show, or opera and they are not familiar with the piece, I give them the context. Then we discuss why the words chosen were used. (1929, 87)

There are many songs from the twentieth century that I would like to use as examples, but I also do not want to run afoul of copyright lifetimes that have recently become radically extended. Therefore, I'll use a timeless favorite from the nineteenth century. I'll also mark up a song of my own composing. You'll find both at the back of the book.

Let's consider a famous tune that many believe to be an old Irish folk song. In truth, many of the songs we think came from Ireland were written in the United States, and often not by people of Irish heritage. Being of Irish ancestry myself and knowing both authentic and American-Irish songs, I am the first to say that the Irish are a maudlin people. Many songs are of death, and even more are of unhappiness. If you doubt this, recall the words of the most famous and beloved Irish song, "Danny Boy." The Irish extract great beauty from the emotionality of sorrow, and my personal conviction is that this race is so acutely aware of the precious gift of life that they deplore its tribulations and end. Some believe that "I'll Take You Home Again, Kathleen" is about a man singing over the body of his wife who has died of grief, pining for the *auld sod*. This is not true. In fact, it has a happy thread: once Kathleen is home, "all your grief will be forgot." Read the verse and the chorus. Therefore, this song should not be sung as sorrowfully as most sing it.

PHRASING

We turn yet again to the venerable Garcia for his opinion: "What is phrasing? It may be simply to carry out the musical punctuation, or it may be, taken in a wider sense, to give each phrase its proper effect in the general conception of a piece" (1894, 51).

Garcia goes on to say that "In rhythmical music, four bars (less commonly three, and more rarely still two) constitute a musical phrase.... Two consecutive phrases may form a sentence or period." I don't know if we must be that hidebound about it, but there is certainly a periodicity in much vocal music with which we all feel comfortable. We are very used to four plus four measures forming a unit for singing.

In "I'll Take You Home Again, Kathleen," we note the repetition of melodic phrases. Garcia is correct that the first complete phrase is four bars, with a comma at the end of the second, which allows for a breath. The next phrase begins with the same music but alters its second half, for variety and so that the melodic line can climb. Good music is good for sound reasons. In this instance, the weaving up and down suggests the undulations of waves and mountains, connoting distance. Note also how the accompaniment in the right hand is a series of broken chords that waver and suggest tedious forward movement or perhaps the roll of the ocean. Also, journeys have a beginning, a middle, and an end. This song has an arduous climb in the third phrase. For the remainder of the verse, the melody winds slowly downward.

An ancient form that becomes standard in popular and Broadway music of the twentieth century is used in this song. This is the so-called ABA form. The first four measures are the A phrase; the next four are identical to begin and then modify for the sake of variety and are noted as A_1. These two phrases together form a *period.* Now the music changes in shape and height. Although they do not do so in "Kathleen," the melodic rhythmic patterns may also change. This is the *bridge,* or B section. In this particular song, it lasts two phrases, or one eight-measure period. Other songs may only use four measures for the bridge, such as Sondheim and Bernstein's "Tonight." Because "Kathleen" uses the same words for the last eight measures of three verses, it is called a *chorus.* (The music in this book contains only the first verse.) Observe how the accompanying pattern changes in the B section, in fact beginning two measures early. The full chords impede the forward sense somewhat and lend more vitality and excitement. The B melody no longer turns back and forth on itself so relentlessly but rather moves stepwise. Note that the original melody repeats once as A, and then the final four measures bring the song to a close by rising to the highest note, falling an octave, and returning to the tonic note. Predictably, the accompanying pattern also returns to A.

BREATHING IN SONGS

Although the song "Tonight" is somewhat difficult to sing because its compass is about an octave and a half, it is not difficult from the standpoint of breathing. Each phrase is rather short, allowing us to renew the breath without singing to exhaustion. Note here (and in virtually every other piece of vocal music), however, that the composer does not allow enough time for an unhurried breath. If you have ever heard recordings of Irving Berlin, Harold Arlen, Cole

Porter, or George Gershwin singing, you will know why they make no such provision. Composers often have no idea what good singing requires and could care less about allowing time for careful letting in and setting. You, the singing performer, must figure this out.

If you look at an interpretive (edited) edition of any difficult keyboard piece written by Bach, you will see numbers above the notes. These numbers dictate what fingers are best used to play the lines successfully. Likewise, **after going through the lyrics first and then the melody, the singer must carefully note where to breathe. These breaths must be memorized just as the words and melodies are, and must be duplicated time after time. This is no less important than learning the words and music.**

We must husband breaths while singing songs as much as we do during exercises. Lamperti said: "On the art of finishing the phrase with the breath still under control depends the calmness of the singing and largely also the career of the singer" (Shakespeare 1898, 17). This is why I admonish students who have not fully mastered the automatic breath process to sing their songs out of tempo---that is, to pause after each phrase long enough to let in and set the next breath. As their accompanist, I simply wait until they begin again. I have yet to hear that this method has adversely affected their later ability to sing the song at normal tempo. Rather, it has trained their subconscious mind to let in breaths automatically while they concentrate on the musicality of the performance.

The standard mark for a breath is a comma, placed above the vocal line. I personally use as well the notation *BB* when a large breath is required.

For the end of each phrase of "Kathleen," I suggest singing a half-note with an eighth-note tied to it rather than the indicated dotted half. This gives you a full quarter-note, or twice as much time as is indicated by the composer, to let in your breath and set your diaphragm and ribs. In the chorus, I suggest that you mark a breath after the final "home," because two notes of this line are extended (the ones with the dot-and-eyebrow symbol, called a *fermata*). This will allow you plenty of breath to extend the last word. Some accomplished singers will not elect to let in this last breath but rather wish to sing the long phrase as one. This is a matter of personal taste and artistry.

The song "If I Loved You," from Rodgers and Hammerstein's *Carousel,* begins with a very long phrase that should not be divided. Most singers don't breathe well enough to sing the entire second phrase as one. I do not feel that it should be divided up and have always sung it as one. Several fellow singers, as well as conductors, have remarked on how much more artistic sense this made.

In other songs, when no choice is left to you but to breathe swiftly, resort to the *catch breath*. This involves a quick downward pull of your lower abdominal muscles in concert with your normal lowering of the diaphragm. Intercostal breathing will not be possible.

One of the most common errors my students make is falling in love with their long-held notes. It is human nature to want to hold on to anything of beauty, but in the case of sung notes, two problems arise. The first is that the accompanist or orchestra will move on and the singer will fall behind in tempo. Second, at the end of a phrase the singer may hold on so long that she or he has insufficient time to let in and set the next breath. **Do not overhold notes at the expense of musicality or your breath. Plan time for well-let-in breaths.**

Occasionally, a song will be about breathlessness. As an artist, you can portray this quality by releasing partially vocalized breath, but do not yourself be caught without breath. Another aspect of interpretation is expressing fear or surprise. On those occasions, you may wish to allow unused breath to escape with the words to drive the emotionality home. A good example is Schubert's "Elf King" ("Der Erlkönig").

"I'll Take You Home Again, Kathleen," has two rhythmic patterns that the singer may want to modify, and may do so without, I believe, detracting from the composition. These are the pickup eighth-notes at the beginning of phrases. To some, these adversely affect the legato line. Therefore, the last note of the previous phrase should be held only one half, a quarter-note of silence is used for the breath, and the pickup note will be a quarter-note. The second consideration is in measure 8, where the sixteenth-note "rocks" the line too much. Instead, the previous note may be held as two beats of a triplet and the last note the final triplet.

LEGATO

Shakespeare says of legato,

> The word "*legare*," meaning in Italian "to join," gave rise to the term "legato style," and signifies a high class of singing, the attainment of which advances the singer to the front rank of his art. He must be able to join one note to another in such unconscious freedom, that no jolt or smearing between the different sounds can be felt or heard. There should be no "seeking for," or "feeling for," the note.... Notes sung legato have been said to resemble pearls on a string, the string being the breath. (1924, 54–55)

Because "Kathleen" is a love song, we can expect that it should not be sung rapidly. **Singing legato means singing with maximum emphasis on the vowels. In general, we extend the initial vowel of each word as long as** possible and place any final consonant directly before the following word. Remember that the Old Italian Masters said, "He who cannot join the notes cannot sing."

Example from "Kathleen": "A-cro---ssthe o-cean wi-ldan---dwi-eed."

If I wish to remind myself to sing a passage particularly smoothly, I will place a long, curving line (a phrasing mark) over those words. I may also do this to warn myself that the line is long and will require extra breath control.

TEMPI

Tempo simply means "time," or the speed of a piece or section of a piece, and *tempi* is the pleural. The songwriter has instructions for us at the start of most songs. This is quite common. Instructions of tempo and expression may change within the piece if the mood is not the same throughout. In "Kathleen," we see "Andante con Espressione." Such directions are either given in the language of the composer or in Italian, which is the most universal written language for music. This one means "walking with expression."

Here are common Italian phrases for tempo and mood:

lento	very slowly
con allegria	with happiness
largo	slowly
con brio	with élan
andante	walking
furioso	furiously
andante cantabile	walk at singing speed
espressione	expression
andante con moto	walk with impulse
con abbandono	with abandon
allegro	with speed
più mosso	a little more; faster
vivo	sprightly
presto	fast
prestissimo	very fast

We may also see:

⌒ or ⌣ , which are *fermatas*. These indicate holding the note, generally for about double the note value. Also, we may see the abbreviations *rall.* and *rit.,* for *rallentando* and *ritardando.* These mean to slow down the section until you see the sign *a tempo,* which means to go back to the original tempo. You may wish to put these into the music yourself, if that is your interpretation. **Always be sure that your accompanist's copy of the music has all your markings.**

Longer songs, and more dramatic songs, frequently have changes of emotion, and with these often come changes in tempo. The mere length of a song may dictate that the pace should not be the same throughout. Keep this in mind as you analyze songs.

Finally, be aware that changes from soft to loud or vice versa may tempt you to alter tempi when this is not indicated. If you are not following a conductor, you are expected to maintain the correct tempo yourself.

FINISHING CONSONANTS

Be sure to enunciate, without overemphasis, final consonants. Include the "n" in "been," the "d" in "bride," and the "k" in "cheek." Do not sing "nuh," "duh," or "kuh," but merely include the pure consonant.

DYNAMICS

Even the shortest song suffers if there are not some changes in intensity of sound. Most composers include notes on their intent in this regard. In this composition, Westendorf wishes us to begin medium loud and then increase to loud at the bridge. Here are the common symbols for intensity:

p = *piano,* soft
pp = *pianissimo,* very soft
mp = *mezzo piano,* medium soft
ppp = very, very soft
sp = suddenly soft
mf = *mezzo forte,* medium loud
f = *forte,* loud
ff = *fortissimo,* very loud

fff = very, very loud

sfz = *sforzando,* suddenly forceful

fp = *forvepiuno,* quickly from loud to soft

There are also the "hairpin" symbols:

< crescendo = become louder

> diminuendo = become softer

The length of these symbols indicates how quickly or slowly such swelling or softening should occur.

You may also see the following:

˙ over a note. This means to accent it or sing it short and detached.

ˇ this also indicates accent and generally indicates more forcefulness than the dot.

If such marks are not indicated, or if you wish to interpret differently than is indicated, you should write this on all copies of the music.

In general, when a note is held a long time, it should undergo some dynamic change. Perhaps you will allow it to fade away. Often you will swell it gently in the middle and then fade back. This is done to keep the sound from becoming boring.

APPROACHING HIGH NOTES

"In a musical figure I *must place the lowest note in such a way that I can easily reach the highest*" (Lehmann 1924, 51–52).

"Kathleen" is a beautiful blending of *conjunct,* or stepwise, and *disjunct,* or jumping, tones. The very first phrase covers the distance of a ninth. Moreover, for most singers, it will go through the break in the voice. This means that the singer must be ready and not surprised. Mark especially difficult jumps on your music. The rubric for these is to **always think of the highest note in a passage and prepare your resistance accordingly. Do not forget the important maxim "When we sing up, we think down."**

Often, long phrases will climb or jump to high notes. It is here that singers most often "crack" or "break." The reasons are twofold. The main one is that they have not let in enough breath or have not held enough back to keep the pressure up. When the air pressure falls, the jaw and throat try to compensate and lock up the windpipe area. The second reason is that the singer has not set the strong muscles "down" sufficiently from the beginning to balance that needed abdominal pressure. The singing system becomes unbalanced, and the voice cracks.

Also remember that simply because a note is high does not mean that it must be sung loudly.

As Cooke wrote in the introduction to his 1828 collection of exercises, "Beware of being flattered into the belief that a strong and powerful voice is to be preferred; many persons are known to sing loudly, but few sweetly."

SILENCE IS GOLDEN

Few amateur singers understand that silence is as important to music as sleep is to life. The so-called pregnant pause has great impact in music. To hear a wonderful example, find a recording of Barbra Streisand singing "Free." It's a song wherein the lady protests too much and too frantically about her joy at finally being free of a romantic relationship. We know just how unhappy she is at the end of the song when she sings, "Free again; free again … free." Streisand not only uses extra breath to make her note sad and without energy, but she waits longer than a lesser singer would dare to speak/sing this last, telling word.

Note composer indications for silence, and be aware yourself of opportunities to use this tool to enhance performance.

STRESS AND ACCENT

Stress and accent are actually two different techniques in singing. The accent is abrupt. Stress is longer, affected by pitch, duration, and intensity. Generally, you accent a word or syllable; you stress a line or phrase.

Good lyricists know how to write their words with inherent musical rhythms. The words that need stress almost always fall on the downbeat of the measure or the secondary beat (in common-time music, on the first and third beats). You will often find the verbs, adjectives, and adverbs falling in these places. Whatever the scheme, you as performer must calculate which words are most important and will be accented or stressed. Not everything can or should be made important.

Lerner and Loewe's *Brigadoon* is filled with beautiful, touching music. In one song, the baritone lead tells his sweetheart just how much her love means to him. He sings about having watched several lonely men in his life. Now he realizes that "*There* … but for *you* go I." These are the downbeat and secondary downbeat words. Moreover, most good singers place a fermata over the "there" to further accent it, because this is the fundamental message of the song.

In the bridge of the first verse of "Kathleen," we hear that "The roses all have left your cheek / I've watched them fade away and die / Your voice is sad when e'er you speak / And tears bedim your loving eyes." The naturally accented words are *roses, all, cheek, watched, fade, die, voice, sad, speak, tears, dim,* and *eyes.* I think you will agree that these are the more important words of these two phrases.

KEEPING TONES HIGH

Constantly strive to make your tones resonate in the mask. This can be a problem with some words. The sound "*y*" is particularly problematic. *You* is a common word in songs, and there are *yets* and *yearns* and *yours.* A pure "y" is made low in the throat. Substitute "ee-oo." "R" is also a concern. The word *heart* provides a good example. This "ur" sounds low in the throat. Sing instead "hot" with just a touch of "r," and note the higher resonance. In general, if you think of the way Italians and the "propah" English pronounce their words, you will sing with more resonance.

WORD PAINTING

Accomplished lyricists use charged or image-rich words to transfer their intent. They may employ onomatopoeia, alliteration, or other techniques, and you as performer should be aware of these and give them their due. Stephen Sondheim is a nonpareil lyricist and tunesmith. His "I Remember" from *Evening Primrose* contains especially effective word painting: "When the wind would blow" has three *w*'s that invite extra breath. "Leaves … crisp as paper" features hard consonants that should be emphasized.

CHAPTER 12

Performance

VISUAL ARTISTS HAVE STONE OR CLAY FOR SCULPTURE, canvas and oils for painting, or film or megapixels for photography as mediums to transmit their visions. In ballet, the performer is supported by music, sets, lighting, and costumes, but his or her body is the essence of conveying intent in this art form. The singer as artist falls somewhere in between, because she or he has the awesomely affective advantage of words. Nevertheless, the use of the body and the shading of the voice often make the difference between a merely competent singer and one who truly moves audiences. This chapter explores the performance and particularly the use of the body to augment the impact of words and music.

ELEMENTS OF PERFORMANCE

INTENSITY AND EMOTIONALITY

"Intensity is the basis of all expression in singing," writes Shakespeare (1898, 48). Another word closely aligned with *intensity* is *focus*. Neither necessarily must mean forcefulness or loudness. Sometimes, when someone is very, very angry, he or she goes beyond shouting to whispers hissed through clenched teeth. The point here is that you must understand your individual potential and attitude toward expressing intensity. Some singers, such as Dean Martin, Perry Como, and Bing Crosby (the crooners), as well as Gordon Lightfoot, Judy Collins, or Enya, have little intensity in their delivery. Their mainstay is

singing a song with a pretty voice and making it sound beautiful, breezy, and easy. However, their performance style also limits them, and they rely heavily on the meaning of the words and the shape of the melodic line for impact.

For some singers, their limit of intensity is a matter of lung power. Other singers are able to sing with physical intensity but not with effective emotionality. It is not in their personality to expose their inner selves that much. Some people sing because they have lovely voices. Others need to express themselves. Another class needs to draw affection from audiences. The reason that Judy Garland and Marilyn Monroe inspired such rabid fans was that they made clear their need to be loved. They exposed their vulnerabilities and put everything they had into performances.

"Whatever characteristics the singer's style may disclose, his singing will be convincing only as it emanates from his real personality" (Fucito 1922, 207).

As I stated earlier, it is extremely important to "know thyself" as a performer and why you need to sing. You may be a rather formal, reserved person who cannot let out all your emotions in front of an audience. Or you may not be able to become someone else, to slip into a character very unlike yourself. History records many singers who have had a bit of success singing and then tried to step beyond their limitations and fallen on their faces. I personally recommend stretching one's limits when a performance is not that critical, such as taking the mike on a karaoke or coffee house night and trying a tune or style you've never done before. You may pleasantly surprise yourself with your willingness to incorporate your emotional self into songs and "let it all hang out."

On the whole, you should take a good, long, honest look at yourself and your talents and build repertoire and characters conducive to who you are and whom you can comfortably turn yourself into, not whom you wish you could be. There are so many songs and so many roles that a number of them are sure to be right for you. What is certain is that if you don't understand who you are, your audiences and those you audition for will decide for themselves. They will let you know, one way or the other.

CONTROLLING EMOTIONALITY

"Emotional expression is relative and not a matter of excessive force [so that] small voices can express as intense emotion as large voices, though of course not with the same degree of physical force" (Russell 1904, 8).

It is no coincidence that *artificial* has the word *art* in it. So does *artifice*. Art is not natural; it is controlled. Often, this control is used to create something more beautiful or powerful or impressive than normal life. A frequent goal in art is to touch the audience emotionally. To do this, the artist must affect emotionality. This is not the same thing as becoming emotional. Many emotions, such as rage, anger, jealousy, and fear, produce physical states that will undo a singer. I have seen on two occasions, at the vaunted Metropolitan Opera, singers who allowed themselves to be carried away by the emotion of the moment and who lost their breath control and then began to clamp down on their throat muscles. In each case, within a few minutes the extreme vocal demands of the piece, the huge orchestra they had to be heard over, and the enormous house they had to project into had them too hoarse to continue to the next act.

Part of art is making the unreal appear real. For the singer, it is to appear to be within the thrall of pure emotion while still being in physical control and balance. As someone in the arts has said, "That's why they call it acting."

BODY EXPRESSION

"The artist on the operatic stage or the speaker on the platform, without facial expression begotten of muscular activity, may lessen by half his power over the audience" (Fillebrown 1911, 15).

Even in formal classical concerts, with the singer anchored near the grand piano, while the audience is listening to words and music they are also looking at the performer. They are consciously and unconsciously trying to pick up clues as to what they should be feeling about the piece.

The first and most important rule of body expression is that the singer should be in control of all his or her movements. Less is more. There must be no extraneous, unintended motions. Just as in dramatic theater, the audience makes the assumption that everything that happens on a stage is intended toward the artistic end. Nervous gestures are especially noticed. Tension and anxiety will immediately transfer to the audience. Even the cocking to one side of the head or the flicking of thumb over fingers is picked up by the audience. Look at yourself in the mirror to catch such things. Better yet, get someone you feel can be objective to watch a rehearsal.

Most clues for how you should be using your body in support of the music come from the words of the song itself. For example, while you're waiting for the introductory four measures of "Soon It's Gonna Rain" to be played, it might be wise to look slightly upward at the "sky," as if appraising the weather. If you're singing the lyrics "Who told you you're allowed to rain on my parade?" you might well thrust an accusing forefinger out at someone in the audience. You might pat your chest when singing, "I'm gonna love you like nobody loves you, come rain or come shine." For the first song, you might look wistful, the second, forceful, the third, warm and loving. Remember that the eyes are the windows of the soul. Remember also how much mystery the Mona Lisa conveys with that slight smile. Humans are capable of picking up very subtle clues from faces, even at a distance.

Sometimes songs have subtexts that must be conveyed, as with the song "Free," in which the singer exults long and loud about the joy of losing a lover. The modal (major and minor key) and tempo changes in the music convey the irony to the careful listener, but when an artist visually allows the manic mask to disappear, showing a depressed soul behind it at the end of the song, the effect is wonderful.

One major problem many of my students have is lack of conviction. This is evidenced by making half gestures. I ask them to indicate the rainbow mentioned in a song, and their hand goes out only far enough so that their elbow can stay safely anchored against their chest. Half gestures look halfhearted. Only if the song's character is wishy-washy do these work. This does not, however, mean that the gesture must always be made swiftly. If you are singing the long phrases in *Oklahoma* about the corn growing high, your hand should rise slowly, not as if the corn has sprung up like Jack's beanstalk. If you can't bring yourself to believe in the gesture or to produce it naturally, sing your song without it.

In general, the singer should stand tall, on straight legs but not on locked knees. The body should have the weight over the front foot. If you are singing to another character on the stage, learn to "cheat out." This means to divide your focus, so that the line from your nose to the horizon should point halfway between the other actor and the audience. If instead you stand in true profile, most of your sound will go into the wings and not to the audience's ears. Audiences understand this convention and absorb it without effort.

For some reason, people who have no trouble whatsoever letting their hands hang at their sides in real life often have the worst time leaving them there during performances. I have found that the trick is to relax the entire arm out of the shoulder socket and to roll the shoulders back slightly Let the relaxation extend down to your fingertips. If you have a nervous nature, find a nonnoisy prop, such as a pair of gloves or a handkerchief, to hold to secure your hands.

Remember that the mark of a true professional is to focus the audience's attention on that which it should be watching. This means no upstaging by talking or making any superfluous gestures that might distract the viewers when you are not singing or reciting. The best actors help the audience by riveting their attention on the speaker or action.

MAKE IT LOOK EASY

"A perfect voice speaks so directly to the soul of the hearer that all appearance of artfully prepared effect is absent" (Taylor 1908, 12).

The mark of any artist is to make the performance look spontaneous, fresh, and, above all, easy. By *easy* I mean that the real person is not seen struggling with the character, and every song has a character behind its words. I also mean that unless the role calls for agitation or anguish, the singer should in general look relaxed and at ease. This goes hand in hand with the technical studies in the front of this book. The more in control of your singing instrument you are, the more at ease you will be. This control is both physical and mental. If you do not believe you will get to the end of the song freely and powerfully, your attitude will show not only in your voice, but also in your body language. When all is said and done, public singing is entertainment. Audiences do not want to suffer along with you vicariously unless you are playing a part like Joan of Arc. To make it look easy, you must be willing to put in bundles of time working on the boring aspects of technique. There is simply no time during performance to concentrate on stance, breathing, and articulation. It's like being provident in your financial life: the more money you put into the bank, the more you can afford to live on the interest.

GETTING THROUGH THE SONG

It is amazing how easy a song is to remember in practice and how much trouble it can be under performance stress. I have evolved my own techniques for helping me. Songs can have difficult leaps, key and meter changes, long phrases requiring extra breath, passages with slightly altered melodic lines, difficult successions of words, and other challenges. As I practice, both alone and with an accompanist, I never allow myself to make the same mistake more than twice. The moment I repeat a gaffe, I isolate that area and practice it over and over. That does not mean, however, that I might not forget this or other things in performance. To help further, I imagine a garden clothesline. Hanging from each imagined clothespin is something that requires my attention. As I cannot dwell on it because I have so much more to do, once I get to the moment I imagine plucking the concern off and dropping it into a waiting basket. In the course of one song, I might have two phrases with similar words that I must keep straight and two places where I need to let in large breaths. I find that when I have definite points to concentrate on, inchoate fears fade away.

If a song is particularly long or difficult, I preach working on the end first and working methodically backward, so that the piece ends stronger than it begins.

FEAR

Franklin Roosevelt was not the first but the most famous for saying, "The only thing to fear is fear itself." This adage may be too simplistic for real life, but it is generally true under performance conditions. If you are a professional singer who has developed laryngitis, you have something to fear in not lasting strongly through the performance. In a more general sense, fear only makes performing worse. If you have done your technical work faithfully, if you have studied the music and words well and have the equivalent to my mental clothesline well established in your mind, you will do fine. Remember that audiences are there to have a good time. They want you to do well and understand that "to err is human."

As Bacon puts it, "Conquer any alarm which may seize you on going to sing by recollecting the general goodwill of society, and kind reception which the public always bestows on merit; remember also that every hearer is not a judge" (1824, 51).

In fact, most people understand that the spontaneity of live theater comes at the price of less than perfection. Brian Stokes Mitchell meant to say "gypsies" during a Broadway performance of *Man of La Mancha*. Instead, in a moment of mental inattention, he found himself saying "Egyptians." He laughed, and the audience laughed with him. As Nanki-Poo in *The Mikado,* I once had a pigeon fly down from the rafters and strut back and forth upstage while I was singing a love song to the soprano. Breaking character to see what was making the audience laugh was not possible, and I just sang on and played my part. The audience felt so sympathetically for what my feathered rival had done to me that I got tumultuous applause for the rest of the evening. It's only entertainment. Keeping that fact in mind should shrink your fears to realistic proportions.

Like idle hands being the devil's workshop, fear works best when you are standing in the wings with nothing to do, waiting to perform. The answer is to fill your thoughts slowly and carefully by reviewing what you want to accomplish when you begin performing.

Fillebrown suggests, "Let in many deep breaths to relax." He has another good solution. "As a yoga master would do, practice deep breathing. Relax your muscles by creating the balance of pressure and resistance. Stand as you wish to once on the stage. Lengthening one's body also has a calming effect" (1911, 27).

FINAL ADMONITIONS

If you are acting in a musical, opera, or operetta, you must learn from the director if his or her intent is to keep up the "fourth wall." This means for all the actors to pretend that there is a wall between them and the audience and not to make eye contact, to play to the audience, or to react to them other than to space out delivery between laughter, applause, and other noisy reactions. If the fourth wall is to be broken or if you are in concert, you will ingratiate yourself to the audience if you let your eyes settle on one, two, or even a small group from time to time. They will feel as if you are singing to them alone. When appropriate to the mood of the music, a smile goes a long way toward creating favor.

When not making eye contact, it is best to imagine the horizon at the back of the performance venue and focus there. This keeps your head and neck on a plane most conducive to good singing.

If you don't have a conductor or band leader, you will have to cue the accompanist when you want to begin. This is generally done with a small nod of the head.

If, during the introductory music or any final accompanying phrases when you're not singing, unless you have some stage business that will enhance the mood and piece, stand quietly and either look to the horizon or down a few feet in front of you, as in the depth of thought that either prompted the song or will prompt the next words.

And learn how to bow gracefully. You deserve the applause.

EXERCISE SHEETS

Exercise I   Pulsated, staccato

hah   hah   hah   hah   hah   hah   hah   hah   ha.

Exercise IA   Pulsated three step

ho   ho   ho   ho   ho   ho   ho   ho   ha.

Exercise 2   Resonating in the mask

hung - oh,   hung - oh,   hung - oh.

Exercise 2A   Plus three step

hung - ay,   hung - ay,   hung - ay. _____

Exercise 3   Connecting tones

yah   no   yah   no   yah   no   yah   no   yah.

Exercise 3A   Disjunct tones

yah   no   yah   no   yah   no   yah   no   yah.

Exercise 3B   Adding legato steps

yah   no   yah   no   yah. _____

EXERCISE SHEETS

ah ——————————— ah ———————— ah.

Exercise 5   Free tongue and lips

dah   may   nee   poh   tu   lah   hay.

Exercise 6   Pure, high vowels

me   may   mah   mow   moo.

Exercise 6A   Pure vowels, reverse order

moo   mow   mah   may   me.

Exercise 7   Agility

la la la la la la la la la la la la   la la la la la la la la la la la.

Exercise 8   Messa di voce

nee. _____

Exercise 9   Agility and smoothness

lah. _____

Exercise 9A   With more articulation

lay ___ lay ___ lay ___ lay ___ lay.

Exercise 9B   Smooth and detached

lah ____ lah ____ lah ____ lah ____ lah lah lah lah lah.

Exercise 9C   Full octave

day ____ day ____ day ____ day ____ day day day day day.

Exercise 10   Octave legato, fifth staccato

lah ____ lah lah lah lah la.

Exercise 10A   Octave legato and staccato

lay ____ lay lay lay lay lay.

Exercise 11   Octave leaping

noh noh noh nay nay nay nah nah nah nah na.

Exercise 11A   Articulation

mah may mah mah may mah mah may mah may ma.

Exercise 12   Extending the line

noh ____ noh noh no.

Exercise 13   Increasing agility

lee ____ lee ____ lee.

SAMPLE SONG 1

I'll Take You Home Again, Kathleen

Words and Music by Thomas Westendorf, 1876

SAMPLE SONG 2

Who Was I?

Brent Monahan © 2003

looked in - to his face.

ANNOTATED BIBLIOGRAPHY

Appelman, D. Ralph. 1974. *The Science of Vocal Pedagogy.* Bloomington: Indiana University Press. Appelman was for several decades the leading vocal scientist on the famed Indiana University School of Music faculty.

Bach, Albert Bernhard. 1898. *Musical Education and Vocal Culture.* 5th ed. London: Paul Trench, Trubner.

Bassini, Carlo. Ca. 1857. *Bassini's Art of Singing: An Analytical Physiological and Practical System for the Cultivation of the Voice.* Boston: Oliver Ditson.

Behnke, Emil. 189?. *The Mechanism of the Human Voice, with a New Chapter on Voice Failure by Mrs. Emil Behnke.* 12th ed. London: J. Curwen and Sons.

Botume, John Franklin. Ca. 1897. *Respiration for Advanced Singers.* Boston: Oliver Ditson.

Brown, William Earl. 1931. *Vocal Wisdom: Maxims of Giovanni Battista Lamperti.* Boston: Crescendo Publishing.

Burgin, John Carroll. 1973. *Teaching Singing.* Metuchen, NJ: Scarecrow Press.

Caruso, Enrico. 1913. *How to Sing: Some Practical Hints.* London: John Church. Caruso (1873–1921) was considered the greatest Italian tenor of his time. This book is generalized and too incomplete to serve as a guide. It is filled with reminiscences.

Clifton, Arthur. 1846. *Clifton's Vocal Instruction.* 3rd ed. Philadelphia: George Willig.

Clippinger, D. A. 1929. *Fundamentals of Voice Training.* Boston: Oliver Ditson.

———. 1932. *The Clippinger Class-Method of Voice Culture.* Bryn Mawr, PA: Oliver Ditson. Clippinger (1860–1930) was an American choral conductor, singer, and teacher. He studied voice in London with Shakespeare.

Cooke, James Francis. 1921. *Great Singers on the Art of Singing.* Philadelphia: Theo. Presser.

Cooke, Thomas Simpson. 1828. *Singing Simplified in a Series of Solfeggi and Exercises Progressively Arranged with an Accompaniment for the Pianoforte.* New York: William Hall and Son. Cooke (1782–1848) was an Irish conductor and later singer who moved to London and taught at the Royal Academy of Music.

Corri, Domenico. 1810 or 1811. *The Singer's Preceptor, or Corri's Treatise on Vocal Music.* London: Chappell.

Crowest, Frederick James. 1914. *Advice to Singers*. 10th ed. London: F. Warne, 1900.

Downing, William Bell. 1927. *Vocal Pedagogy for Student, Singer, and Teacher*. New York: C. Fischer. Downing was for twenty years professor of voice at the University of Kansas.

Duey, Philip A. 1951. *Bel Canto in Its Golden Age: A Study of Its Teaching Concepts*. New York: King's Crown Press. Mr. Duey wrote the book in reaction to music psychologists who held that knowledge about the singing mechanism could not be made useful to improve other singers. He also wished to record a history of early voice teaching in Europe.

Fields, Victor Alexander. 1947. *Training the Singing Voice: An Analysis of the Working Concepts Contained in Recent Contributions to Vocal Pedagogy*. Morningside Heights, New York: King's Crown Press. This book was the pioneer compendium reference work on publications concerning the singing voice, covering the years 1928–1947.

Fillebrown, Thomas. 1911. *Resonance in Singing and Speaking*. Boston: Oliver Ditson. Fillebrown considered the use of resonance to be the most important factor in good singing.

Fucito, Salvatore. Ca. 1922. *Caruso and the Art of Singing, Including Caruso's Vocal Exercises and His Practical Advice to Students and Teachers of Singing … with Ten Portraits and Caricatures*. New York: Frederick A. Stokes. Fucito was Enrico Caruso's coach and accompanist from 1915 to 1922. The book exercises are enlightening, but half the book is biography.

Garcia, Manuel, II. 1847 and 1872. *A Complete Treatise on the Art of Singing: Part Two, the Editions of 1847 and 1872*. New York: Da Capo Press, 1975. Garcia (1805–1906) was the most celebrated voice teacher of the nineteenth century. He was the son of the Rossini tenor Manuel Popolo Vincente Garcia. Among his pupils were Jenny Lind, Henriette Nissen, Mathilde Marchesi, Charles Santley, and Henrietta Sontage.

———. *Hints on Singing*. 1894. New York: E. Schuberth.

Henderson, William James. 1906. *The Art of the Singer: Practical Hints About Vocal Technics and Style*. New York: G. Scribner's Sons.

Lablache, Louis. 184?. Boston: Oliver Ditson.

Lamperti, G. B. 1905. *The Technics of Bel Canto*. New York: G. Schirmer. Giovanni Battista Lamperti (1840–1910) was the son of Francesco Lamperti, a professional singer, and an exponent of his father's teachings, which he claimed he could "trace back to the Italian singing-master Gasparo Pacchierotti (d. 1821), Giovanni Battista Velluti (d. 1861) and others."

Lehmann, Lilli. 1924. *How to Sing.* New York: Macmillan. Lehmann (1848–1929) was the greatest German dramatic soprano of her time. She was taught by her mother, Marie, a leading soprano at Kassel.

Lunn, Charles. 1888. *The Philosophy of Voice.* 6th ed., enlarged. London: Bailliere, Tindall, and Cox.

Mackenzie, Sir Morrell. 1891. *The Hygiene of the Vocal Organs: A Practical Handbook for Singers and Speakers.* 5th ed. New York: E. S. Werner. Sir Morell Mackenzie was Physician to the Royal Society of Musicians and consulting physician to the Hospital for the Disease of the Throat, in London. The book's first edition, produced by Macmillan and Company in London, appeared in 1886.

Marafioti, Pasqual Mario. 1925. *The New Vocal Art.* New York: Boni and Liveright. This teacher's knowledge is diminished by his lengthy attacks on other teachers and methods.

Marchesi, Salvatore. 1902. *A Vademecum for Singing-teachers and Pupils.* New York: G. Schirmer. Marchesi (1822–1908) was a Sicilian nobleman who sang baritone professionally and studied with Lamperti and Garcia.

Martens, Frederick Herman. 1923. *The Art of the Prima Donna and Concert Singer.* New York: D. Appelton. This book interviews professional singers and elicits their opinions on vocal production and performing.

Melba, Nellie Mitchell. 1926. *Melba Method.* London: Chappell. Nellie Melba (1859–1931) was an Australian dramatic soprano of great fame. She studied with Mathilde Marchesi in Paris. All her fundamentals are presented in seventeen pages, followed by vocalises and exercises.

Muckey, Floyd S. 1915. *The Natural Method of Voice Production in Speech and Song.* New York: C. Scribner's Sons.

Myer, Edmund J. 1891. *Vocal Reinforcement.* Boston: Boston Music Company.

———. 1911. *Position and Action in Singing.* 8th ed. Boston: Boston Music Company.

Nathan, Isaac. 1836. *An Essay on the History and Theory of Music; And on the Qualities, Capabilities, and Management of the Human Voice.* 2nd ed. London: Fentum. Nathan (1790–1864) was an English composer and tenor, who studied under D. Corri.

Owsley, Stella. 1937. *Helpful Hints to Singers.* Dallas: Dealey and Lowe.

Panofka, Heinrich. Ca. 1859. *Gesangs—A B C.* Leipzig: J. Reiter-Beidermann.

Pfeiffer, Michael Traugott, and Hans Georg Nägeli. 1830. *Auszug aus der Gesangbildungslehre nach Pestalozzian Grundsätzen.* Zurich: H. G. Nägeli.

Reid, Cornelius L. 1950. *Bel Canto: Principles and Practices.* New York: Joseph Patelson Music House.

Rushmore, Robert. 1971. *The Singing Voice.* New York: Dodd, Mead.

Russell, Louis Arthur. 1904. *Some Psychic Reflections for Singers.* Newark, New Jersey: Essex Publishing.

———. 1905. *English Diction for Singers and Speakers.* Boston: Oliver Ditson.

Scheidemantel, Karl. 1910. *Voice-Culture.* 2nd ed. New York: Breitkopf and Härtel.

Seiler, Emma. 1900. *The Voice in Singing.* Philadelphia: J. B. Lippencott.

Shakespeare, William. 1898 and 1910. *The Art of Singing.* Boston: Oliver Ditson.

Stanley, Douglas. 1916. *A Few Remarks on Voice Production and the Operatic Timbre.* Montclair, New Jersey: n.p.

Taylor, David Clark. 1908. *The Psychology of Singing; A Rational Method of Voice Culture Based on a Scientific Analysis of All Systems, Ancient and Modern.* New York: Macmillan. Taylor (1871–1918) was the American dean of singing teachers of his period. He was a graduate of the College of the City of New York. He was a strong proponent of watching and imitating.

Thorp, George E., and William Nicholl. 1896. *A Text Book on the Natural Use of the Voice.* London: R. Cooks. Nicholl was a professor of singing in the Royal Academy of Music.

Van Broekhoven, J. 1908. *The True Method of Tone Production.* New York: H. W. Gray.

Wronski, Thaddeus. 1921. *The Singer and His Art.* New York: D. Appelton. Wronski was an operatic bass.

INDEX

CD TRACK LIST

CONTRIBUTOR CREDITS: **SOPRANO,** Cathy Liebars
MEZZO-SOPRANO, Christy Altomare
TENOR, Brent Monahan
BARITONE, Robert Lenzi
BARITONE, Douglas Tester
PIANIST, Douglas Tester
COMPILER AND MIXER, Reese Altomare